BRIEF TO COUNSEL

(NEW EDITION)

BRIEF TO COUNSEL

BY

HENRY CECIL

*(His Honour H. C. Leon
formerly one of Her Majesty's
County Court Judges)*

Illustrated by Edward Ardizzone, R.A.

With a foreword by
THE RIGHT HON. LORD DEVLIN
*Formerly one of Her Majesty's Lords
of Appeal in Ordinary*

London
MICHAEL JOSEPH

First published in 1958 by MICHAEL JOSEPH LTD
52 Bedford Square, London, W.C.1
SECOND IMPRESSION SEPTEMBER 1958
THIRD IMPRESSION SEPTEMBER 1958
FOURTH IMPRESSION NOVEMBER 1958
FIFTH IMPRESSION JUNE 1962
THIS EDITION 1972

7181 0997 x

*Set and printed in Great Britain by
Tonbridge Printers Ltd, Peach Hall Works, Tonbridge, Kent
in Baskerville eleven on thirteen point on paper supplied by
P. F. Bingham Ltd, and bound by James Burn
at Esher, Surrey*

CONTENTS

LIST OF ILLUSTRATIONS

FOREWORD

A YOUNG man who wants to go to the Bar usually starts
thinking about it when he is coming towards the end of
his schooldays or is at the beginning of his university
career. If he does not come of a legal family it will not
be easy for him to find out the sort of things he wants
to know before he finally makes up his mind. He will
get an introduction or two, I dare say, to a barrister or
a judge and make the most of a half-hour interview.
But he would be very lucky if he got anyone of real
experience to tell him as much and to tell it to him as
pleasantly and as informatively as Mr Cecil does in this
book.

When it was first published fourteen years ago, there
was still for most young barristers a period of briefless-
ness during which they learnt the job by watching how
the regulars did it. As Mr Cecil says in his preface to
this new edition, the situation in this respect has greatly
changed. Like most changes it is a mixture of good and
bad. It is good in that it mitigates the hardship of
poverty and discouragement which deprived the Bar

of many young members who, if they had stayed, would have distinguished themselves and their profession. It is not so good in that it diminishes, if not obliterates, an invaluable apprenticeship. I am glad that Mr Cecil makes this point so forcefully. Three years theoretical and six or twelve months practical is too short by the standards of most professions. It is hard to expect the young barrister, anxious to win his spurs, to let slip what may seem to him a glittering chance. It is the barrister's clerk, the father-figure to whose wisdom the profession owes so much, whom we must now rely on to see that the newly-called learns to walk before he starts to run.

But whether the period of watching and waiting be long or short, the watcher must know what to observe and how to profit by his observation. That is the great value of this book. For those who like to read about the law at work, it is first class entertainment: for the would-be barrister who really wants to know it is all that and first class instruction as well. Every law student who is thinking of the Bar and who wants to be told about it and has no high-minded objection to being amused in the process, should begin by reading this book.

DEVLIN

Author's Preface to New Edition

SINCE this book was first written fourteen years ago there have been dramatic changes in the fortunes of the Bar. In 1958 it was still one of the most difficult professions at which to succeed and one in which initial progress was probably slower than in any other profession. If the reverse is not now the case, it is very nearly so. The reason is not in doubt and provides an outstanding example of cast bread returning, and after not so many days at that.

Before the first Legal Aid and Advice Act was passed in 1949 there had been schemes for free legal aid in civil cases and for poor prisoners' defences but one cannot pretend that many successful practitioners at the Bar took much part in them. However, when Parliament introduced the new Legal Aid scheme the Bar accepted it, though it did not at first realise the tremendous advantage to the profession which this new aid would bring. Legal Aid was to be properly paid for and subsequent Acts greatly increased the number of people who could obtain it.

In 1958 Legal Aid was just beginning to improve prospects at the Bar though at first only very slightly. But the movement gathered momentum after 1958 and within a few years of the first edition of this book being published it became plain that, coincident as the new scheme was with the unfortunate increase in crime, prospects at the Common Law and Criminal Bars were going to become far better than they had ever been in the history of the profession.

But it is very much to be hoped that the fact that it is now comparatively easy for newly-called barristers at the Common Law and Criminal Bars to gain a substantial income early in their careers will not result in a decline in the standards of integrity, advocacy and industry in the profession. I have added some suggestions in the hope that they may help some young people to avoid the dangers and pitfalls inherent in a too-easily won practice. If they are not avoided, the result may be that in the end our standards of integrity and justice will sadly deteriorate.

In the original edition I wrote that 'one day there may be a rule that no pupil shall be allowed to appear in court until after he has read for a year in chambers'. At that time he could appear in court on the first day after which he was called. For some years now there has been a compulsory period of six months' pupillage before appearance in court is permitted. I realise the practical difficulties in the way of extending this period to a year, but I still hope that it will happen. In many cases the present rule is unfair to those represented by a six-month-old pupil. I refer to this matter again in the chapter called 'Pupil'.

There have been other changes in the English legal world since 1958 and I have tried to bring this book fully up to date, though so popular is the Bar becoming as a profession that probably the figure for practising barristers which I give (2,800) will be too low by the time this book appears.

1 *The Way Ahead*

CRIMINALS sometimes refer to barristers as mouthpieces. Although mouths are certainly used a good deal at the Bar and on the Bench (and sometimes too much in both places) you need more than a mouth if you want to become a successful barrister. The object of this book is to tell you, in as cheerful a manner as the subject allows, whether you have any chance of becoming one and what you are likely to experience in the process.

Some suggestions will also be made with a view to accelerating the process. The road used to be narrow and slow. It is much wider and faster now. But, as indicated in the preface to this edition, there are serious dangers in too high a speed limit. Moreover, there are still plenty of obstructions and there are ditches not only on both sides of the road but in the middle. Many of them are unlighted and have no warning signs and, if this book supplies a red light here and there and a notice or two, it may be of some use to you. You cannot expect the legal authorities to put 'Black Spot' outside a difficult judge's court, although the idea is an attractive one. 'Fog Service after lunch' might well have appeared outside the court of a certain judge, now dead some years. Others you will think of as you go along. 'Dead Slow' for example, or 'Roundabout Ahead.'

It is to be hoped that your reason for wanting to go to the Bar is not that you 'love a good argument'. Most people who say this are incapable of logical argument and mistake word-quantity for word-quality. They seldom give you a chance to complete a sentence and, when they do, they do not listen to it but are busily preparing their next outflow. On these occasions you will usually observe a glazed look on their faces much the same as that on the face of a person at a party who is tired of you and wants to meet someone else.

In the first edition of this book I gave as an example of a poor argument the following dialogue :

'What I say is, they wouldn't be in prison if they hadn't done wrong.'

'Well, of course not, Mrs Smithers, but don't we want to prevent them from doing wrong again when they come out?'

'But everyone knows he shouldn't steal.'

'Quite, Mrs Smithers, but once a man has stolen and gone to prison don't we . . .'

'Serve him right, I say.'

'That may be, Mrs Smithers, but isn't it to our advantage if . . .'

'To have people stealing? Certainly not. The Government do enough of that. Only last week my husband had another demand from the Income Tax. It's bare-faced robbery, and with fares going up.'

'I wasn't suggesting that it was to our advantage to have people stealing, Mrs Smithers. What I wanted to say was—isn't it desirable not simply to punish a man for doing wrong but to help him not to do it again?'

'He knew he oughtn't to do it the first time.'

'No doubt he did, Mrs Smithers, but wouldn't it be better if . . .'

'Well, he got what was coming to him, that's all, I say. Now I really must be going. Thank you so much. It's been delightful. If there's one thing I do enjoy it's a good argument. Some people say I ought to have been a barrister.'

I don't think that this is a very good instance of a bad argument. Mrs Smithers had her point of view, which was that people shouldn't steal and that they should be punished when they did. She obviously came from the school which thinks of the victim rather than the offender. While some people think that criminals should be treated differently from the way in which they are now treated there was nothing illogical in the stand which Mrs Smithers took. But she would not have made a successful barrister for another reason. She would not listen. In order to be able to argue successfully you have got to listen carefully to what the other person says.

A little later on, the qualities which you ought to have if you are likely to succeed at the Bar will be suggested but first you must know how to set about becoming a barrister and what it is going to cost you.

Your first step is to become a student at one of the Inns of Court of which there are four—Lincoln's Inn, the Inner Temple, the Middle Temple and Gray's Inn. You may choose any one of these Inns and, if you have friends who can advise you as to your choice, you should consult them. In case you have no such friends I shall try to give you as objective a thumbnail sketch of each of the Inns as a member of Gray's Inn can give.

Lincoln's Inn is mainly for those who practise on the Chancery side (see page 53) but being a member of that Inn is no bar to practising on the Common Law side. The present Lord Chancellor (Lord Hailsham), the present Lord Chief Justice (Lord Widgery) and his predecessor (Lord Parker), are all members of Lincoln's Inn, although at the Common Law Bar.

Members of the Inner Temple are more likely to have been at Oxford or Cambridge, although many graduates from these Universities go to the other Inns. You will probably find more wealth and more sons of what used to be called the upper and upper middle classes in the Inner Temple than in the other Inns. The Inner Temple has no monopoly of such members but, if statistics were obtainable, I think that you would find more of them in the Inner Temple than elsewhere. The Middle Temple has the most lovely hall of all the Inns. It is Elizabethan and though damaged in the war, it has been substantially maintained in its original condition. Gray's Inn is the smallest and perhaps the most progressive and friendly of the Inns. (But you must make due allowance for my natural prejudice in this matter.)

There is no nationality bar, but you must comply with certain educational standards. A degree from a university will normally be sufficient, but it is quite unnecessary to wait so long before joining an Inn. You can join on leaving school, provided you've passed sufficient examinations. Normally passes in five subjects of the General Certificate of Education of which two are at advanced level (Grade C or better) will do. But there are other possible qualifications and, as you will have to call at the Inn of Court which you wish to join, you can enquire when you do so whether your educational qualifications are sufficient or whether you will have to take a further examination to qualify for admission. Alternatively if you live abroad you can write for the information. You will find the Sub-Treasurer of the Inner Temple and the Under-Treasurers of the other Inns most helpful when you make your enquiries.

You will also have to give references as to good

character and pay fees amounting to £82. You may also be required to deposit £100 on admission but this may be waived in whole or in part and is not normally required from University students. On call to the Bar a further fee of £75 must be paid.

You must not be engaged in any paid occupation which is not approved by the Benchers of your Inn, but today almost any honest occupation would be permitted, other than working in a solicitor's office. Even this may be allowed subject to certain conditions.

You must be over 21 when you are called to the Bar and there is no upper age limit. Some older people go to the Bar after having been in another job or in business. If they have the ability, there is no reason why they should not succeed and their previous experience may be of great value. A very few barristers become solicitors first and a high proportion of those who do find their way to the High Court Bench. The present Lord Chief Justice started his professional career as a solicitor.

After admission as a student it will take you three years at the least (it should not take you more) before you can be called to the Bar. During those three years (unless excused wholly or in part by your Benchers) you must attend at your Inn three times in each of the four legal terms in each year and eat a dinner. If you want to be excused from eating the full number of dinners you should apply to the Sub-Treasurer or Under-Treasurer of your Inn as the case may be. When I joined Gray's Inn in 1920 each dinner cost 3/6d and this included wine. After my first dinner I told my father, who was interested in wine, what we had to drink. I said that it was a red wine and that it was called Château Lafite 1899. He wondered if it was too late for him to become a student. It has not been possible to maintain this standard and the price of the dinner has gone up to 25p plus a term fee of £1. The other Inns charge rather more.

Eating dinners is an admirable and traditional custom by which you get to know fellow students and possibly barristers and begin to feel the atmosphere of the Bar. That atmosphere is essentially a friendly one and dinners are an admirable way of being introduced to it. Many years ago there was much more association between the Benchers and senior barristers of an Inn on the one hand and the students on the other than there is today. Some students complain that they have to come a long way to eat their dinners and that they only meet fellow students when they do. Although discussions with fellow students have their value, as does the introduction to the traditions of each Inn, it is a pity that there is not the same association with senior members as there used to be. Three times every two years each Inn has the use of Cumberland Lodge in Windsor Great Park for a week-end. During these week-ends students do get to know barristers and judges and other benchers and not only listen to lectures and have formal legal arguments but meet their seniors informally too. This is invaluable but unfortunately there is not enough of it.

What is important is this. One of Britain's great assets is a Bench and legal profession which has a very high standard of integrity. This is partly the case because the barrister's profession is a very small one, and the judges are mainly selected from the Bar. Owing to the small number of barristers and the association between them, the standard of integrity and ability of possible candidates for the Bench is known to the profession as a whole. Consequently no one who is not of the required standard of integrity is ever appointed. The result is that the personal behaviour of judges in their privates lives is almost without exception beyond reproach. There are no rules of conduct laid down for judges because none are required. This is very different from the situation in the United States of America where there are thousands of judges and where from time to time they suffer from a justifiable lack of trust in some of their judges.

During the three years while you are eating your dinners you will also be taking the necessary legal examinations. I deal with these in a later chapter. There are numerous scholarships available during your studentship, apart from State scholarships. For some an examination is required, for some only your means and past record are considered. They vary from a small award to a sum which will not only pay all your fees, including your pupillage fee, but will also provide you with a useful annual income during your first three years at the Bar. Particulars of all available scholarships can be obtained from each of the Inns and, if you want a scholarship, you should write for particulars.

In the result, in order to be called to the Bar you must be able to keep yourself for three years either out of your own or your parents' resources, out of scholarships or out of such paid occupation as the Benchers of your Inn may permit, you must pass your examinations and you must pay altogether £157. You can then be called to the Bar and you must then read in the chambers of an experienced junior barrister as his pupil. (For the meaning of a 'junior barrister' see p. 156.) Some barristers no longer charge fees for pupillage but where a fee is charged it is £115.50 (including a fee of £10.50 to the clerk) for a year or half that amount for six months. You are only *required* to read as a pupil for six months but it will be most unwise of you not to read for a year. That is a short enough time in which to learn how the legal wheels go round.

After six months' pupillage you will be entitled to appear in court and to accept briefs of your own. But in six months you will have learned nothing like enough to justify your practising and it is highly desirable that you should devote the second six months to learning. But there is a problem here, particularly in criminal chambers. Owing to the amount of work available it must be very tempting to a newly-called barrister, particularly if he is married, to take all the work he can get. It is therefore quite possible that a pupil of six months' call will have so much work of his own that he will have no time to go round with his master and learn how the work should be done. The temptation to go after fees rather than tuition must be very great, but in the long run it will be much more beneficial to learn how the job can be done well rather than to accept money for doing it badly. This is easy advice to give but difficult to take. Nevertheless the wiser among you will divide their time at least equally between learning and practising. They will earn less during the six months than their more grasping brethren but they will be laying up for themselves treasure on earth. It is difficult to find chambers in which to become a pupil and it is to be hoped that barristers who take pupils will do so on the understanding that a pupil will devote the greater part of his time to learning as a pupil. I have no doubt that this will be insisted upon in good Common Law chambers. But in chambers which specialise in criminal work it will be difficult for all concerned to resist the temptation of using the pupil to do briefs for which there is no one else in chambers available.

Although prospects at the Bar are infinitely better than they used to be, this is far less noticeable on the Chancery side or in a practice which excludes all criminal work. It is nevertheless to be hoped that newly-called barristers of the highest quality will not be tempted to go for the immediate rewards, if their natural inclination is to practise, for example, in the Chancery division.

Of those who start to practise it used to be the case that about 1 in 4 gave it up at a fairly early stage. Today the proportion is probably much smaller in view of the better prospects which now exist. Legal Aid has certainly come to stay and it looks as though such better prospects will continue.

The gross income which it is possible for you to earn as a barrister is large, i.e. as a highly successful junior from £8,000 to £20,000 and as a highly successful Q.C. from £12,000 to £35,000. The incidence of taxation on large incomes, however, makes this prize far less worthwhile from a purely acquisitive point of view than an ordinary salary or profits from a business. Barristers are allowed no entertainment or similar allowances and if they dine at expensive restaurants it is paid for by themselves, not by the public. So the glittering prizes of wealth which used to be available for barristers no longer exist. But as against this a reasonable income can normally be earned as soon as pupillage is over. After that year anything from £1,500 to £3,000 a year can be earned at once. At the criminal Bar progress may be even faster. Here is an example of the first six years' practice of a barrister called in July 1963.

1964	...	...	...	£344
1965	...	...	...	£1,200
1966	...	...	...	£2,500
1967	...	...	...	£3,250
1968	...	...	...	£4,000
1969	...	...	...	£5,500

This young man was in Common Law chambers. In criminal chambers his progress might have been considerably faster.

It may be interesting to compare those figures with those of a junior who was called to the Bar in 1923 and who left it after (excluding the war years) twenty years' practice, when he was earning fees at the rate of about £7,000 per annum.

1st year (while a pupil)	...			£39
2nd year	...	...	...	£41
3rd year	...	...	...	£150
4th year	...	...	...	£200
5th year	...	...	...	£400
6th year	...	...	...	£800

And here is a later example of an able young man's experiences before crime and Legal Aid came to the help of the Bar.

1948 (while a pupil)		...		£70
1949	...	...	...	£600
1950	...	...	...	£900
1951	...	...	...	£1,400
1952	...	...	...	£1,700
1953	...	...	...	£2,200
1954	...	...	...	£2,900

Under the 1956 Finance Act it was provided that the purchase of a deferred annuity by annual premiums not exceeding 10 per cent of the earned income could be treated as an expense for tax purposes with a maximum of £750. Rather better provision was made for older barristers.

A barrister is not legally entitled to his fees. He has no legal remedy if he is not paid. The remedy in practice is in the hands of your clerk who will refuse work from solicitors who are known to be bad payers, unless they pay in advance. It used to be the case that in a barrister's early days he was likely to incur a number of bad debts in this way. Today the incidence of bad debts is much less. This no doubt is partly due to the fact that a good deal of a barrister's work is done under the Legal Aid & Advice Act. So solicitors are able to look to the Legal Aid Fund for payment and not to their sometimes impecunious clients.

Normally the minimum fee which a barrister will receive today is £2.50. This includes the clerk's fee. Until comparatively recently the barrister was paid not only his own fee but a fee for his clerk. But this practice has now been abolished and every fee includes the clerk's fee as well. I deal with barristers' clerks' fees and remuneration in a later chapter.

The ordinary fee on a brief in a modest-sized High Court action (other than divorce) will vary from £30 to £250; in the County Court from £3 to £45. Short defended divorces usually attract a fee of anything from £12.50 to £30. Undefended divorces take place in the County Court and attract a fee of normally £12.50.

A fee on a High Court brief is for the first five hours of the case, which is a legal day. For every subsequent five hours or part of five hours the barrister is entitled to a refresher fee. The amount of this varies and it is normally about half to two-thirds of the original fees marked on the smaller briefs. Different considerations apply to the larger cases, e.g. where the brief is marked £500 or more. In the County Court a refresher is paid for each day.

So today a barrister can earn from £1,500 to £3,000 in his first year after pupillage and after that according to his ability it may go up quite quickly to from £5,000 to £10,000. How different this is from the situation less than twenty years ago. In an article by a *Times* Special Correspondent published in that newspaper on the 13th August, 1953, it was stated that the average income of juniors of three years' standing was under £250 per annum, that the average income of those of five to nineteen years' standing was under £800 and of those of twenty years' or more standing £2,700. One of the few consolations for the young barrister of those days was the fact that they were some of the few people described as 'esquire' who were entitled to be so described. They still are.

If your object in going to the Bar is to become a judge the prospects have improved. In 1958 there were about 150 judges, including County Court judges and Metropolitan and Stipendiary magistrates. In 1971 there were between 200 and 300 and there are now about 350 full-time and 275 part-time judges. There is a danger that this may lower judicial standards and it is suggested that it would be better for the Government to abolish the trial of road-accident cases (which are pretty hit-or-miss affairs anyway) and deal with them by way of national insurance. Less than 300 judges would then easily cope with the remaining work and their standard would be unimpaired.

A substantial part of a junior's income is made out of the preliminary work before an action comes on for

Barristers in Court
or
'My Learned Friend may affect indifference'

trial. This preliminary work consists not only in advising but in drafting the technical documents required in the case and in appearing on applications relating to the trial of the action. These applications may be for a temporary injunction, or for an order that the other side must produce certain documents or deliver particulars of allegations it has made, or for any purpose which may enable the action to be fairly tried when it comes on for hearing. Some of these applications are little more than formal, others may be of great importance and might eventually go on appeal to the House of Lords, though this is very rare.

Quite a number of people become barristers without intending to practise. And it is possible to give practice a trial with a view to going into one of the legal departments of the Civil Service if success at the Bar does not come quickly enough. Indeed, some barristers, who have given up practice, have done exceptionally well and attained positions of the highest importance in the Civil Service.

Some industrial concerns have legal departments where barristers who have given up practice can be employed. In addition there are, of course, top-grade positions taken by eminent barristers on retirement from the Bar. This book, however, is written mostly for the benefit of those who wish to succeed at the Bar and not for those who do not really intend to practise.

2 *The Four Qualities*

A SUCCESSFUL barrister requires four qualities. First and foremost he must have the ability to understand quickly what is said to him and the patience to listen to it. Secondly he must have the ability to express himself in simple and intelligible language. His sentences must have a beginning middle and an end. If he can develop an attractive style, so much the better. But this is not vital. What is essential is that everything he says should be easy to understand. If, for example, you cannot do better than Mr Crabtree, do not go to the Bar. Here is Mr Crabtree opening a case:

'My Lord, in this case I appear for the plaintiff and my learned friend, well, I will tell your Lordship about my learned friend in a few moments—actually before I start opening the case it is necessary for me to tell your Lordship that the plaintiff or rather his wife, at lease I am not sure but it was one of them, while the plaintiff or his wife was walking down the street near their house, well—I am not sure if it was there— actually it was while they were both in the garden when somebody from the next house on the right, it may have been the left—no I think this was a telephone conversation, however it will be absolutely clear if your Lordship will look at the correspondence at page 3—oh, your Lordship hasn't got the correspondence—well I will have it handed up to your Lordship and if your Lordship would look at page 3—no I think it's page 13-

no actually it was a telephone conversation, when my client the plaintiff was talking to the defendant or to the defendant's wife—no that was in another case I'm afraid. But while he was actually on the pavement and walking along his wife came out and said something to him which I must not tell your Lordship because it is not admissible in evidence—it is a vital part of the whole truth as a matter of fact which the plaintiff is going to swear to tell, but nevertheless I must not tell your Lordship, but as your Lordship has the correspondence—actually it is in the pleadings—probably it is put better in paragraph 7 of the Statement of Claim. No, it's in paragraph 8 of the defence I think, my Lord. I am so sorry not to be quite clear on this subject but, my Lord, actually this case came into the list rather unexpectedly and I was on my feet in the Court of Appeal and I was told by my clerk that your Lordship was sitting and so I had to ask the Court of Appeal for leave to come to appear before your Lordship and they very kindly said I could leave them at once—I was almost in the middle of a sentence—it was very good of them and I hope I haven't kept your Lordship waiting too long but, as I was saying, the plaintiff was on this pavement or in the garden, well whichever it was, he was there or was it his wife—one or other of them was there when the policeman came and—no, that was a running down case—I'm so sorry my Lord, I am thinking of the case in the Court of Appeal, but, as I was saying my Lord, I appear for the plaintiff in this case. . . .

JUDGE: It seems a long time since you first told me that, Mr Crabtree.

CRABTREE: Surely not, my Lord, that is all I have told your Lordship.

His Lordship
or
'Is that your best point?'

JUDGE : I know but it seems to have been a long time.

CRABTREE : I am so sorry my Lord but if your Lordship would bear with me. . . .

Well, the judge must be left bearing with him as well as he can. Why the Crabtrees of this world ever come to the Bar no one ever knows. Why anyone briefs them is an even greater mystery. But, if for no other reason than charity to the poor judges who have to sit and listen, don't go to the Bar if you're likely to be a Crabtree.

So these are the first qualities required—patience, a quick understanding and the ability to say clearly what you mean. The other two qualities are integrity and a capacity for hard work.

Integrity is very important. It is quite true that there are a very few criminals who might have made a good living at the Bar but they are very, very few and their careers might have come to a swift and inglorious end at any time. The Bar is essentially an honourable profession. It is not, as is sometimes supposed, an alibi factory for criminals. The shysters of American films do not exist at the English Bar. You will occasionally come across a man who, if the truth were known about him, could be disbarred but who manages to break the rules without being demonstrably found out. Such men are rare and have little success. In short, a barrister does not invent a case for a client; he puts forward the client's case to the best of his ability. The question 'What do you do when you know your client is guilty?' is asked of lawyers so often that a separate chapter will be devoted to it.

Capacity for hard work is essential. There are a few sports who get by on a minimum of work but ninety-nine per cent of those who succeed at the Bar have had to work probably harder than in any other profession at one stage in their career. And that stage lasted a good many years. So, if you're not prepared to get down to it, if you have too many outside interests, if you rather fancy yourself as a novelist or playwright, go to the Bar by all means if you wish but don't imagine that you're likely to succeed in that profession. If all you want is material for your books or plays you will find some no doubt, but, if you do not devote at least the first seven (and preferably the first ten) years of your life at the Bar solely to that profession, you will be unlikely to succeed.

A most valuable personal qualification for the Bar is to be a good loser and to accept setbacks without complaint and without attributing them to causes outside oneself.

Good health is essential, as a barrister is entirely dependent on himself. A man of indifferent health may easily become a successful solicitor but it is almost impossible to be successful at the Bar without, at any rate, initial good health.

3 *On Examinations*

IF you have the four qualities mentioned in the last chapter you are likely to succeed at the Bar. But unfortunately today it is possible to succeed without them. In the years before the first edition of this book appeared it was possible to fail at the Bar even if you had the four qualities mentioned, unless in addition you had either luck, scholarships, goodwill among one or more solicitors or alternatively private means. But private means was sometimes the undoing of a promising young man, for, even though you may have the capacity for hard work you may not make use of it if you can live and enjoy yourself without doing so. There have been several able young men who would probably have succeeded at the Bar but for their misfortune that they did not need to earn a livelihood. Today success at the Criminal Bar and to a lesser extent at the Common Law Bar is mainly contingent on your finding satisfactory chambers. Once you are installed in such chambers you are likely to succeed unless you refuse to work or are particularly stupid.

Much of the original chapter on examinations has had to be re-written. Roman Law has at last been abolished as a subject. In England it was almost purposeless except in so far it was an exercise for the mind, and for years there have been far better exercises for the minds of prospective barristers than that. The Bar final examination is now a more practical examination than it used to be. Examinations of the type now set will be of more value to the student. They involve the application of law to facts and provided the examiners are of a sufficiently high calibre to enable them to judge the quality of the students examined, they will make a considerable advance in legal education. The measure of success of this new method, however, will not be satisfactorily evaluated until there has been sufficient experience of the examiners and the examinees. More important than the examinations themselves is the tuition that leads up to them. If this is done well, examinations should be unnecessary. Those who conduct the practical examinations should be able to judge whether the student has reached a stage which justifies call to the Bar, just as in the old days students were called to the Bar without any examinations at all when it was thought that they were fit to be called. It is probable, however, that for many years written and oral examinations will continue and will be felt necessary for the training of barristers. So you have got to pass them. But your real training will not begin until you have been called to the Bar and start to read as a pupil.

Scholarships, apart from the fact that they will enable you to live, are of some use in that in certain cases by gaining them you will at the same time have gained a little more knowledge of the law than those who have not attained the same standard. But don't be misled by them. Many of those who do extremely well at examinations do very badly at the Bar and many of those who only scrape through in the third class do extremely well. The truth is that, however much you cram your brains with law, you cannot tell the extent of your ability to apply that knowledge until you are in actual practice. And it is the application of knowledge

of law and procedure that counts, not the possession of
it. The important thing for all students to do is to try to
grasp the principles of law. It is most unlikely that they
will succeed until they see the law working in practice
but, if they try from the start, it will be a help.

Of course the attainment of a high academic standard
can be of use in other ways. For example, if you fail
at the Bar, you can go in for teaching law or your
qualifications may help you when you go into one of
the legal departments of the Civil Service. But, if
your set ambition is to practise at the Bar, don't worry
too much about scholarships (unless you *have* to gain
them) or a high standard in your examinations. Do
rather more than enough work to get through them at
the first attempt and meanwhile learn as much as you
can about your fellow men and any other subject which
interests you—whether it is motor-car engines or garden·
ing or architecture. One of these days you may have a
case where your outside knowledge will be very helpful
to you.

Until about 1700 there had been a very strict educational system for prospective barristers, though there
were no examinations in the modern sense. But between
1700 and 1852 students went round with barristers in
much the same way as pupils do today. They went into
court and heard the arguments and then at night in
hall after dinner they argued about cases which they
had heard during the day. In other words their tuition
was entirely practical and they did not have to pass
any specific examination. During those 150 years we
had as good judges as we had before then and as we
have now. As judges were appointed entirely from the
Bar it does not appear that there was very much wrong
with that system of education. Nevertheless examina-

Descent from the Robing Room
or
One for each day of the week

tions as we know them today started on a voluntary basis in 1852 and became compulsory in 1872.

I should qualify my remark about the amount of work you should do for your examinations by adding that it looks as though it would be worth your while to work hard at the new practical final examinations. You will find these far more interesting than ordinary examinations and, if the standard of lecturer or tutor is high enough, you may well find that the work you do for them stands you in good stead when you start practice at the Bar.

This advice is, of course, intended for the average student, who might attain a second class pass if he sacrificed the rest of his student life but would be unlikely to obtain a first class. It is not suggested that potentially great lawyers or those who take such an interest in pure law that they want to learn as much as possible, should put a brake on their studies.

You must not, however, assume that because you have done very well in your examinations you will do well at the Bar, even in arguing a point of law. There is all the difference in the world between the ability to learn and repeat such principles of law as are plainly established and the ability to apply those principles to the facts of a particular case. Moreover, there are many matters of law which even to this day have never been satisfactorily settled. The possession by you of a 'certificate of honour' by no means ensures that when one of such matters has to be argued, you will do it justice or get justice for your client.

For the purpose of theoretical examinations, for the most part you merely store up knowledge of cases which you believe to be authority for certain propositions. For the purpose of giving an opinion or arguing a case you have to throw away preconceived ideas and look up every case which may conceivably shed light on the matter. From time to time you will come across statements in text books of high authority which, when carefully examined, turn out to be wrong. It is no good just telling the judge : 'My Lord, it says so in Halsbury,' unless Halsbury[1] is right and you are able to show that it is right and why.

[1] Halsbury's *Laws of England.*

4 *A Chapter of Explanations*

THIS chapter is going to be rather heavy going, and it should probably be skipped by any reader who merely wants to be entertained. Moreover, most of the information in it will be elementary to lawyers and even to some law students, though the latter may pick up a hint here and there, e.g. how to address judges out of Court. Its object is, as far as possible, to enable anyone interested to understand the various words and phrases used in this book and to have a general picture of the legal edifice in England.

(i) *The Courts*. The Courts Act 1971 has altered the structure of the Courts. It has abolished Assizes and Quarter Sessions and created the Crown Court to take their place. And it has created the new 'Circuit Judges'. All judges of County Courts are now Circuit Judges and have jurisdiction in addition to their County Court jurisdiction.

There are two main bodies of law in England— civil and criminal. Civil law deals with private disputes between individuals or firms or companies or occasionally between individuals or companies and the Government. Criminal law deals with crime.

Here is a table of the Courts. Their functions are described below. The list of civil matters dealt with by the Crown Court and Magistrates' Court is not exhaustive, though it is enough for the purposes of this book.

CIVIL

1. House of Lords.
2. Supreme Court (consisting of :
    (a) The Court of Appeal.
    (b) The Chancery, Queen's Bench and Family Divisions of the High Court.
    (c) The Crown Court (e.g. in connection with rating and highway matters and appeals in civil matters from Magistrates' Courts).)
3. County Courts.
4. Magistrates' Courts (e.g. in connection with separation and maintenance disputes between husband and wife, affiliation orders and actions for possession of land).

CRIMINAL

1. House of Lords.
2. Court of Appeal (Criminal Division).
3. The Crown Court.
4. Magistrates' Courts.

The Family Division of the High Court now exercises the jurisdiction previously exercised by the Chancery Division in wardship cases. So in the High Court the welfare of children is dealt with in the Family Division. The Chancery Division now exercises the jurisdiction previously exercised by the Probate Division in contested will cases. Many actions can be brought in either the Queen's Bench or Chancery Division but for the most part the Queen's Bench Division in fact deals with the ordinary litigation you read about, breaches of contract, accident cases, libel actions and so forth. The Chancery Division is more concerned with the interpretation of trusts and wills and settlements, with partnership and with the purchase of land. It also deals with the winding up and re-construction of companies. Certain actions cannot be started in the County Court, e.g. libel, but apart from these special cases the County Court deals with all ordinary litigation, though normally it cannot try cases where more than £750 is involved, except by consent. The Court of Appeal hears appeals from the High Court and the County Court. A very few civil or quasi-civil matters are dealt with by the Crown Court.

Magistrates' Courts are presided over either by a Metropolitan Magistrate (in London only), a Stipendiary Magistrate or unpaid Justices of the Peace. Every criminal case, large or small, starts in the Magistrates' Court, and many (such as motoring offences, petty stealing and the like) finish there too. In more serious cases the accused is committed by the Magistrate for trial by jury at the Crown Court, if it is considered that there is a case against the accused.

The Crown Court replaces Assizes and Quarter Sessions. The more serious cases will be tried by a High Court Judge in the Crown Court and the less serious cases by Circuit judges. About 275 new part-time judges called Recorders will also hear some of the less serious cases in the Crown Court. There used to be about 175 barristers, also called recorders, who presided at Borough Quarter sessions four times a year. These have been replaced by the new Recorders who have rather wider powers.

The Court of Appeal (Criminal Division) sits in the Law Courts to hear appeals from the Crown Court. The Central Criminal Court (The Old Bailey) which used to be the Assizes for London is now part of the Crown Court. The titles of the Recorder of London and the Common Serjeant of London still remain, although these Judges are Circuit Judges.

(ii) *The Judges and how to address them in and out of Court.* Here is a table of the full-time judges and most of the judicial officers in England and Wales.

They are all permanent appointments, except that of the Lord Chancellor, who is a member of the Government and changes with it. The appointments of Chancery Master and Registrar and County Court Registrar are made only from solicitors. Nearly all other appointments are made solely from the Bar, but solicitors are eligible to become Recorders and Recorders of 5 years' standing are eligible for Circuit Judgeships. The duties of a Master are described later.

The total number of full-time judges and judicial officers is a little over 500 of which about 160 are Masters or Registrars.

A few members of the legal profession do not know how to address judges when they meet them out of Court. A barrister would speak to them like this :

'Good morning, Lord Chancellor.'

'Good afternoon, Lord Chief Justice' or 'Good afternoon, Lord Chief.'

'Good evening, Lord Stone.' (Law Lord.)

'Good night, Master of the Rolls.'

'Good day, President.'

'Goodness gracious, Lord Justice.'

'Good for you, Judge.' (High Court or Circuit Judge.)

'Goodbye, Recorder.' (or 'Common Serjeant') (see the last sentence on page 40–41).

Every barrister calls his colleagues (whether Q.C.s or juniors), however eminent they may be, simply by their surnames.

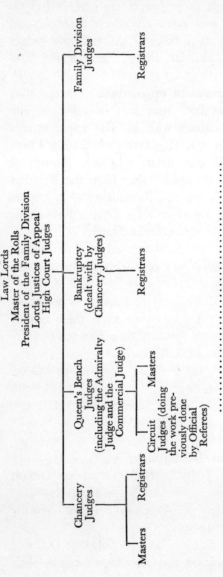

Lord Chancellor
Lord Chief Justice
Law Lords
Master of the Rolls
President of the Family Division
Lords Justices of Appeal
High Court Judges

Chancery Judges

Masters　　Registrars

Queen's Bench Judges (including the Admiralty Judge and the Commercial Judge)

Circuit Judges (doing the work previously done by Official Referees)　　Masters

Bankruptcy (dealt with by Chancery Judges)

Registrars

Family Division Judges

Registrars

Circuit Judges (including the Circuit Judge known as the Vice-Chancellor of the County Palatine of Lancaster, the Recorder and Common Serjeant of London and the other judges at the Central Criminal Court and the various judges of the Crown Court who have taken the place of Chairmen of Quarter Sessions.)
Metropolitan Magistrates
Stipendiary Magistrates

All High Court Judges and above are either knights, baronets or peers, and members of the public should write to them as, e.g. The Hon. Sir William Robinson and speak to them as, e.g. Sir William. A barrister should in most cases address an envelope to a High Court Judge as the Hon. Mr Justice Brown and to a Lord Justice of Appeal as The Rt. Hon. Lord Justice Brown, and in the letter he would say 'Dear Judge' or 'Dear Lord Justice'. Members of the public should call Circuit Judges when speaking to them either 'Judge' or 'Judge Brown' and when writing, 'His Honour Judge Brown'.

All judges from the High Court upwards (and this includes anyone sitting as a High Court Judge, e.g. Circuit judges or Recorders sitting in the High Court) are addressed in court as 'my Lord', Circuit judges, when sitting in the County Court or Crown Court, and Bankruptcy Registrars as 'your Honour', Magistrates are called 'your Worship' or 'Sir', Masters are called 'Master' and everyone else in the table 'Sir'.[1]

It is impossible and undesirable in a book of this kind to give a detailed account of the duties of the various judges and judicial officers, but here is a short explanation of the work of those whose title does not make their duties seem reasonably plain.

The Lord Chancellor (who has many other duties besides his judicial ones) usually sits in the House of Lords, though he is in fact President of the Court of Appeal. The Lord Chief Justice occasionally sits in the House of Lords but usually sits as a Queen's Bench

---

[1] All judges sitting at the Old Bailey are called 'my Lord' as are the former Recorders of Liverpool and Manchester. All other Recorders are called 'Sir'.

judge, and often presides over the Court of Appeal (Criminal Division). Occasionally he sits in the Court of Appeal in its Civil capacity. Law Lords are either Lords of Appeal in Ordinary (that is, life peers created for the purpose of trying cases in the House of Lords) or peers who have held high judicial office. The Master of the Rolls is President of one of the Courts of Appeal. The Lords Justices of Appeal (who are often confused by the newspapers with Law Lords) form the majority of the judges of the Court of Appeal. They are always made Privy Councillors. They are not peers unless they happen to be so in their own right. Masters are minor judges who deal mostly with the intermediate stages of an action. They mainly decide preliminary disputes between the parties about the conduct of the action before it comes to trial. Registrars in the Chancery Division deal with the drawing up of Orders and discharge other similar duties. In the Family Division the Registrars have duties like those of the Masters in the other divisions. County Court registrars try small cases in the County Court and undertake other duties similar to those of a Master.

(iii) *Miscellaneous Matters.* What is the difference between a barrister and a solicitor : What is a brief, a proof, a lay client and so on?

In England and a few other places the legal profession is divided[1] into two water-tight compartments— barristers and solicitors.

A barrister can only act on the instructions of a

[1] The advantages and disadvantages of the system are referred to (a) in a chapter written by the present author in J. D. Scott's *Life in Britain* published in 1956 by Eyre and Spottiswood (see pages 128–129) (b) in the present author's *The English Judge* published in 1970 by Stevens and Son (see pages 12 to 26).

solicitor, except in the case of a dock brief. Although dock briefs have virtually disappeared, as Legal Aid has for the most part taken their place it is still open to a prisoner who has £2.25 to ask to be represented by any counsel present in court who is not engaged in a case. As in most cases he can get a solicitor and a barrister for nothing, it is not surprising that dock briefs are now virtually extinct. In the Magistrates' Court and the County Court a solicitor can act as an advocate and it is not necessary to employ a barrister at all, though it will often be desirable to do so in cases of substance. In the High Court, however, a person can only be represented in court by a barrister, though he may, of course, appear for himself and not be represented at all.

The position is that, as far as litigation is concerned in the High Court, the solicitor's work is mainly concerned with :

1. Interviewing and taking statements from his clients and other witnesses. Those statements when reduced into writing are known as the 'proofs' of the witness. They usually begin :

'John Jones of 3 Sycamore Gardens, W.1,
WILL STATE——'

Sometimes the expression 'will state' is somewhat optimistic and solicitors could on occasion be excused if they added in brackets 'it is hoped.'

2. Preparing the case for trial under the advice of the barrister he is employing.

The barrister conducts the case in Court, settles most of the technical documents in the case and advises the solicitor as to its conduct. Barristers refer to the documents which they settle and to their written opinions as 'paper work.'

'Counsel' (plural 'counsel') means a practising barrister. There are only two kinds of counsel—junior and Q.C. and the difference between them is described in a separate chapter (p. 156). Treasury counsel are counsel specially appointed to act in some public capacity, e.g. as counsel to a government department or prosecuting counsel at the Central Criminal Court. The junior counsel to the Treasury in the Queen's Bench or Chancery Division is known as the Attorney-General's devil. Treasury Counsel can take private work as well, but neither the Attorney-General nor Solicitor-General may do so. This was not always the case.

Solicitors more often than not work in partnership. Barristers must never do so.

'Brief' means the written instructions sent by a solicitor to a barrister on any particular case. Sometimes they are called 'Instructions' and sometimes 'Case.' 'Brief' is the word to be used for the instructions for the actual hearing of a case or matter in Court or Chambers. 'Instructions' or 'Case' is the word to be used when counsel is only being asked to settle a document or advise.

Chambers has two meanings. Every barrister has chambers. That is the place where he works—his office. Most chambers have several barristers in them but a barrister could have a set of chambers to himself, though in the present state of shortage this is in the highest degree improbable. All practising barristers' chambers in London used to be either in Lincoln's Inn or the Temple. Gray's Inn was considered too far from the Courts. Owing to the shortage of chambers in the

A London Magistrate's Court
or
Older but no better

Temple Gray's Inn does have a few sets of chambers for practising barristers. This was an innovation and has so far not seemed popular. From the point of view of barristers with entirely criminal practices neither the Central Criminal Court nor London Sessions are any more difficult to reach from Gray's Inn than they are from the Temple. But, of course, the Court of Appeal is situated in the Law Courts and this may be the reason why criminal practitioners do not want to go to Gray's Inn. However the shortage in the Temple is so acute that the probability is that Gray's Inn will be used more than it has been in the past.

Chambers also refers to the place where a Judge or Master hears applications in private. There are many intermediate stages of an action which are not heard in public. The room where these proceedings are heard is called 'chambers.' Sometimes they are heard 'in court (as chambers)', i.e. in an actual court but in private.

'The Judge in chambers' refers to the Judge who hears these intermediate or interlocutory proceedings as they are called.

A Master hears similar applications, and he only sits in Chambers. (In the provinces this work is done by a Registrar who is normally the County Court Registrar.) It will be understood that, before an action comes to trial, many things may happen in the preparation of the case. A plaintiff delivers a statement of his claim, a defendant delivers his defence. If the plaintiff thinks that the defendant ought to give further particulars of his defence, and the defendant, when asked, refuses to give them, the dispute as to whether the particulars shall be given is decided in the first instance by a Master. Either side can appeal then to the

Judge. Sometimes the Master tries cases by consent or takes an account between the parties, or fixes the amount of damages to be paid when liability has been proved or admitted.

A barrister is concerned with two people—his solicitor client and the member of the public who is instructing the solicitor; the latter is known as the 'lay client.'

A conference is an interview between a solicitor and barrister (with or without the presence of the lay client) for the purpose of discussing a case. It is normally held in the barrister's chambers and *never* in the solicitor's office. When a Q.C. is taken in to advise, the junior and the solicitor and, if wanted, the lay client attend at the Q.C.'s Chambers, and it is called not a conference but a consultation.

When a barrister starts life at the Bar, he buys a blue bag in which he keeps his robes. Later on, if he is led by a Q.C. and is considered by his leader to have given some useful help in the case, he may be given a red bag by the Q.C. There are plenty of barristers with red bags who have not succeeded very well at the Bar, but there are few[1] successful barristers who have not been given a red bag.

If two barristers are engaged on the same side the senior (if they are both juniors) will 'lead' the other, and, of course, if one is a Q.C. he will lead the junior. A Q.C. cannot appear in an ordinary Court case without a junior as well, except in a case which he has started as a junior and which has come to trial after he has taken silk.

Becoming a Q.C. is called 'taking silk' because the

[1] In the original edition the word 'no' was used. The author humbly apologises to the distinguished few.

gown of a Q.C. is made of silk, whereas a junior's is made of 'stuff.'

A 'pleading' is a written statement of the plaintiff's claim or the defendant's defence, or the plaintiff's reply to the defendant's defence. Occasionally what is called a rejoinder is delivered by the defendant in answer to the plaintiff's reply; the plaintiff can reply with a surrejoinder and there can even be a rebutter and surrebutter to follow. All these documents are known as pleadings and they very rarely go further than a reply. Usually when a party has further information about the case, or second thoughts about it, it is a case for amending his original pleading, not for delivery of a new one.

A 'puisne (pronounced puny) judge' is in effect a High Court Judge. He is often referred to as e.g. Brown J. This means Mr Justice Brown. Brown L.J. means Lord Justice Brown, who is a member of the Court of Appeal.

A solicitor's office consists of the proprietor of the firm or the partners, perhaps one or more assistant solicitors, one or more legal executives, one or more clerks, typists, etc. A legal executive used to be called a managing clerk. He is something less than a solicitor and considerably more than an ordinary clerk. Legal executives have to take examinations before they are entitled to be so called. Many of the old managing clerks had great authority. They acquired in varying degrees knowledge of law and procedure, and, though unqualified by examination, many of them were quite as competent as the solicitor employing them to conduct the whole of an action. There will also be in a solicitor's office articled clerks, that is, young men or women who want to become solicitors and have first of all to serve their articles in a solicitor's office. They used to have to pay a fee for this but the position is now almost entirely reversed. Most solicitors, so far from taking a fee for having an articled clerk, will pay him a small salary, increasing as he passes his examinations. The length of articles will be either three or five years according to the articled clerk's qualifications. There may be a few managing clerks left but they are dying out and their place is being taken by legal executives. For the most part legal executives are better educated than the older managing clerks but it is doubtful if their general skill in conducting litigation is any greater than that of the best managing clerks.

A barrister's clerk, on the other hand, has nothing to do with the conduct of an action. His job is to accept or refuse briefs on behalf of his principals (acting independently for each of them), to arrange the fees, to keep the books, arrange conferences and do what he can to prevent several cases for the same barrister coming on in Court at the same time. He neither needs nor acquires any knowledge of law, nor, except in the most narrow sense, of procedure. Very, very occasionally a barrister's clerk reads for the Bar and becomes a barrister, but this is quite exceptional.

Each Inn is govened by its Masters of the Bench—otherwise known as Benchers. They are members of the Inn chosen for life by the existing Benchers. A member of the Inn appointed to high judicial office is always made a Bencher, if he is not one already. Most of the other Benchers are silks in active practice, but there are always a number of juniors as well.

The word lawyer is used in two senses. A lawyer is a generic term and includes both barristers and solicitors, though when a person says that he will consult his lawyer he means his solicitor. But lawyers use the expression a 'good lawyer' when they are referring to a barrister or a solicitor or a judge who has a high standard of legal knowledge and knows how to apply it. A very well-worn story is that one judge was known as 'Old Necessity' because he knew no law.

5 *Which Branch?*

AT some time before you are called to the Bar you should make up your mind in what branch of the law you want to practise. Common Law? Chancery? Divorce? Crime?

Common Law is all embracing. That is to say, practitioners at that Bar go into nearly all the Courts at some stage of their career. Normal Common Law work includes breaches of contract, torts, landlord and tenant cases, commercial work, libel, slander and so on. But, in addition, bankruptcy, company law, divorce, probate, certain types of litigation in the Chancery Courts and criminal cases may all come the way of the Common Law man. In a sense, therefore, Common Law practice is the hardest job of all because you are not a specialist in anything. On the other hand, it provides great variety and interest.

Chancery work is more concerned with the execution of trusts, construction of wills and settlements, company law, partnership and land and the drafting of legal documents.

As a general rule, if you are more interested in pure law and drafting documents than in advocacy, you should go to the Chancery Bar as opposed to the Common Law Bar, and vice versa. But there are, of course, exceptions to this rule and you can only find out if your case is one by consulting someone of experience.

There are distinguished practitioners at the Divorce and Criminal Bars but it is difficult for a Common

Lawyer to understand why anyone should want to go to either of them. So much of the work there is sordid or monotonous or both. The standard of learning required at those Bars is, however, lower than either at the Chancery or Common Law Bar. At one time very few High Court judges were appointed from the Divorce or Criminal Bars but in recent years there have been rather more of such appointments than previously. It is true that the bulk of the population assume that prosecuting and defending criminals represents the work of the barrister at its zenith. They think that, after you've served your apprenticeship with mere civil cases, you will eventually be allowed to do the really important work of dealing with crime. Then your life will really be interesting, then you really will have your foot firmly on the ladder. Well, that is nonsense. Work at the Criminal and Divorce Bars is undoubtedly easier than that at the Common Law and Chancery Bars. Moreover, although there are sometimes interesting crimes and interesting divorces, the normal housebreaker and thug and the average practitioner in false pretences is a dull fellow. The average matrimonial dispute is dull too.

All the Queen's Bench judges have to take criminal cases. They take them in their stride. The experiment was once tried of sending Chancery judges on circuit—but their stride was rather too long. After the purity of the Chancery Division, they were so horrified when they were brought face to face with real criminals that they imposed astronomic sentences. The experiment has not been repeated.

The Admiralty Bar and the Parliamentary Bar are too highly specialised to need treatment here. If you are already thinking of going to either Bar it will probably be because you have friends or relations

London Sessions
or
'How do I know what he thought?'

connected with one of them, and they will give you all the necessary advice.

There are, of course, sub-divisions among Common Lawyers and Chancery practitioners too. You may find chambers where the work is of the most general description. Alternatively, you may find, for example, in Common Law chambers that most of the work is connected with accidents on the highway or industrial accidents. If you go to such chambers you will find a car, if not a necessity, a very great advantage.

There are, too, specialised chambers where Income Tax or Rating or Town and Country Planning or other specialised work is done, but you are only likely to be able to become a pupil in such chambers through a close personal introduction. Income Tax practitioners in fact never take pupils at all in the normal way.

Some newly-called barristers spend six months in Chancery chambers and then six months in Common Law chambers, with a view either to gaining experience of both or of seeing which they like better. Sometimes a pupil spends six months in general (Chancery or Common Law) chambers and then six months in specialised chambers of the same branch. There is something to be said for taking one or other of those courses but, on the whole, it is probably better to spend the whole year with one master.

Once you are a barrister you can practise in any branch and you can change from one to another or, as many Common Lawyers do, practise in several of them. Some prospective barristers read for a year in a solicitor's office before being called to the Bar. The experience may be very useful but the extra cost and time may prove an insuperable objection for some people.

6 *Choosing A Master*

You are, it is to be hoped, on the threshold of a great career. There was a time when a newly-called barrister knew practically nothing except a little theoretical law. The names of a few leading cases remained obstinately in his head. He had heard of but never met the reasonable man. He had ideas about the way in which offer and acceptance operated so as to constitute a contract. He had probably played about with this problem among his legal friends, writing imaginary letters of acceptance and sending imaginary telegrams withdrawing such acceptance. He had probably heard of the High Trees[1] doctrine enunciated by Lord Denning. He was Denning J. when he first stated it, Denning L. J. when he confirmed it and he now waits in the highest place of all to pronounce his final blessing on it. Your tutors probably expressed their views to you about it and they may have suggested that it was contrary to other higher authority. Well, Lord Denning will deal faithfully with your tutors if and when the case arises. The interesting thing will be to see what the other members of the House will do.

The more practical examinations which now constitute the Bar final examination may make the newly-called barrister more fit to undertake his profession. Nevertheless the vital part is still to come—pupillage. This will be the time when you really start to learn about the law in practice. And you certainly need a

[1] Central London Property Trust Ltd. v High Trees House Ltd. 1947 KB130.

full year's pupillage if you want to equip yourself for this struggle ahead. A year is short enough.

Now who is going to take you as a pupil? It is extremely difficult to find a vacancy. So this is the time for you and your family to be a nuisance to your friends. It is vitally important to you that your pupillage should be spent in the right chambers. So ask anyone you can think of. Get introductions to as many people as possible. Above all try to find someone whose advice appears to be worth while. If you know solicitors on a particular circuit it may be a considerable advantage to you, initially at any rate, to become a pupil in chambers where some of the established members practise on that circuit.

It is so difficult today to find a vacancy for a pupil at all that it is very doubtful if you will have a choice. But if you could choose, probably the best person to go to would be a very able youngish man who is getting on well but has never had a pupil before. But there are not many of them. To be a first pupil of a budding Atkin would indeed be a piece of luck. If you have knowledgeable friends at the Bar ask them if they know anyone who might conceivably be in this class. Not many of you will be accommodated in this way.

The people to avoid are those who *want* pupils. To a busy man pupils as a whole are a nuisance, though every now and then one turns up who makes it worth while. But the really useful pupil is fairly rare. Try hard to be one. If you have the capacity to be one it will be worth any number of briefs sent to you by benevolent and unthinking solicitor uncles.

If you can't become pupil to a man on his way up, try to get in with a really able lawyer, who is not so far advanced that nearly all his cases are large ones.

Entrance to Chambers
or
'I wonder when my name will be up there'

How are you to know one? You can't. You can only do it through your friends. How are you to know whether their advice is any good? You can't. You must trust to luck. And, after all, if you have the intelligence necessary to succeed at the Bar, there is a chance that you may recognise the right sort of person to advise you.

I have already mentioned that some barristers no longer charge a pupillage fee. If it is humanly possible, do not go to someone who will take you because he wants the fee. You will learn little in such chambers and the effect on your future career might be disastrous, or at any rate delaying.

If, before your pupillage begins, the proposed master or his clerk so much as hints that you may be able to stay in the chambers after your pupillage, don't go there as a pupil. It would only be in the most exceptional circumstances arising from close personal relationship that any barrister of ability or his clerk would say anything to a proposed pupil on that subject before he came to the chambers. If he were asked point blank, the answer would be that there could be no possibility at all. Easy vacancies only exist for good reason, viz. that comparatively little work comes to those chambers.

7 *Pupil*

PROBABLY you will not be lucky enough to become the sole pupil to a young man with a brilliant future. The next best thing is to be taken by a junior with a large and varied practice with occasional work in the County Court. This is on the assumption that you are going to practise at Common Law. Naturally if you are going to the Divorce Bar or the Criminal Bar your master will practise almost entirely in the Divorce or Criminal Courts. A Chancery barrister may have rather less work in Court and more drafting in Chambers, and he very rarely goes to the County Court.

You will be in a room with your fellow pupils, and you will probably get on very well with them. The Bar is a friendly profession and the atmosphere in most sets of chambers is a very happy one. There are naturally exceptions to this rule. There are chambers where there are jealousies and backbiting. They are to be avoided. You may work successfully but you cannot work happily in such an atmosphere. Everyone wants to get on, but most people at the Bar are prepared to do so without being jealous of their neighbours who are getting on better and without complaining to the clerk of unfair treatment.

It may happen that pupil A will receive a brief and not pupil B. If this happens several times and the brief has been given to A through the clerk and not because A has a relation or friend who is a solicitor, B may ask himself why he has been left out in the cold. He may go further and ask the clerk. That is not a way to endear himself to the clerk. If the briefs are all directed towards A, there is a good reason for it. Clerks are well aware of the jealousies which can exist in a set of chambers and they do all they can to prevent them. So they will never deliberately ask for trouble. If your co-pupil gets briefs and you don't, don't ask or complain about it. Get on with your work and try to ensure that, when you do get a brief, you will make as little a fool of yourself as possible. Of course, neither of you ought, as pupils, to be allowed to have a brief at all. You are quite incapable of doing justice to it even after six months of pupillage. In 1574 a barrister was forbidden to practise during his first five years after call. In 1614 this was reduced to three years and the rule disappeared altogether somewhere about 1700.

During your first six months as a pupil your work will consist in :

    (i) reading your master's papers;

   (ii) trying your hand at what your master is instructed to do—writing an opinion, drafting a pleading, or making notes for trial, including a note in chronological order of the correspondence and facts to be proved in evidence;

  (iii) looking up points of law which arise during this attempt, or which your master asks you to look up, and making a note of them;

  (iv) going into court with your master;

   (v) taking a note of the proceedings in court;

  (vi) learning from a comparison of your own views with your master's opinion, pleading or conduct of a case—and, if he has time (which isn't often), from his oral criticisms—how and why your standard fell short of that of the experienced barrister.

The whole of your career may be affected by your work as a pupil. And for this reason. It is very difficult for a barrister who has no influence in legal circles to find chambers and the best chance of a successful career after your period of pupillage is to find a seat in busy chambers. Accordingly, if you have become a pupil in a good set of chambers, your object in life during your pupillage is to do so well that you are offered a seat in the chambers after you have ceased to be a pupil. It is useless to mention this subject when you become a pupil. Indeed, as has already been indicated, if any hopes were held out to you of a seat in chambers after your pupillage the chambers should normally be a-voided. But it is easy to recognise even in the early stages of pupillage the pupil who is going to be a really useful devil. There are plenty of devils but very few who are really useful. There is practically no busy junior of intelligence who would not somehow make room in already crowded chambers to keep a pupil who was obviously going to be of great use to him. Conversely, no busy junior is going to add to the crowd in his chambers someone who is only average, unless, of course, there are ties of friendship or relationship.

Accordingly, you must make it your aim in life to try to be useful to your master. If you haven't the ability, you won't succeed, but the work you will have done in trying can only have been to your advantage. But, if you have the ability, you still won't succeed unless you really get down to it. If you are mainly interested in spicy libel cases and in leading a gay social life, no one is going to ask you to stay on in chambers.

Now what must you do? You have already been told that success at the Bar means hard work and your hard work should begin on your first day as a pupil, though it will, of course, be nothing to the work you will have to do later on, if you succeed. First, come to chambers in good time and don't leave early. Don't have lunch engagements away from the immediate vicinity of the Law Courts.

Next, try to understand what is happening round you as soon as you can. It will take a long time. But many people don't even know how to try. For all the trying, there are plenty of things you will never know. The County Court judge who, in a work of semi-fiction[1] said: 'What on earth is a 271?' was no creature of farce. There were at the time of the production of the film quite a number of judges who had no idea what a 271 was.

The only way to learn the practice of the courts is by experience of them *and* by *looking it up*. You learned a certain amount for your examinations. But you only touched the fringe of things, and you will quickly forget all you have learned unless you experience in practice what you have learned in theory and unless, when you have experienced it in practice, you look it up afterwards. Just as some newly-appointed judges have at least a mental picture of a card with 'Shut up' on it facing them on the Bench, so every young barrister should have a card with 'Look it up' on his desk.

If you adopt the invariable course of looking everything up you will eventually learn the practice. And

[1] *Brothers in Law* by the present author, published in 1955 by Michael Joseph Ltd. Adapted for a film of the same name and first shown in 1957.

you won't otherwise. When you go into court and a case begins, counsel for the plaintiff will get up to open the case to the judge. What right has he to do so? Under what rule? Is it an express rule or merely an accepted convention? Look it up. When your master makes an application to a judge to have a case adjourned, why does he make it to that particular judge? Look it up. And don't just be satisfied with a cursory glance. Make sure you have found out the real authority for the practice. If you can't find it, ask for help and don't rest until you've hunted it to ground.

In your master's brief in the County Court you will find perhaps these words: 'Counsel will please ask for judgment for the defendant with costs and will ask for a special direction so as to allow a higher brief fee than that authorised by the scale.' Now your master is a good master. That has been assumed. But, had you been less fortunate, you might well have witnessed the following scene at the County Court.

COUNSEL: Will your Honour certify for a higher brief fee?

JUDGE: What power have I to do that?

COUNSEL: Oh—of course—it's purely discretionary.

JUDGE: Is it? What power is there to do it at all?

COUNSEL: Oh—your Honour has a discretion.

JUDGE: So you say, but under what rule?

COUNSEL: Oh—your Honour, I'm afraid I haven't the actual rule in mind—(fumbles with a green book called *The County Court Practice*).

The next dialogue depends on the nature of the judge. If it is Judge Pleasant he says: 'Let me see the practice. I'll see if I can find it.' If it is Judge Not-too-Pleasant: 'I think you might have taken the trouble to look up the rule before coming here—if it exists. If you want something from the court you ought to know the authority.'

COUNSEL : I'm very sorry, your Honour.

JUDGE LESS-PLEASANT-STILL : Well—I hope it won't happen again. I'll take the next case while you're looking it up. You can mention it later.

And all this to a barrister who has gone so far in his profession that he actually has a pupil. Well—if the pupil has his eyes and ears open he can learn quite a lot from that.

It is quite astonishing how many barristers and solicitors appear in the County Court and ask for something without knowing whether the Court has power to grant it or not. I do not pretend to have been any better myself and my only excuse is that nobody warned me that I must look everything up. At any rate you have been warned and will have no excuse for doing what I did at a very early stage of my career. I had been instructed to appear on behalf of a husband whose wife was claiming a separation order and maintenance from him on the ground of his cruelty. The case was to be heard a little out of London. The instructions in the brief told me the various acts of which the wife complained and the husband's answer to them. But it also said that the parties were still living together. I knew nothing about separation orders in the Magistrates' Court and so I looked up *Stone's Justices Manual* which is the Magistrates' Court practitioner's bible. There it said that a wife could not get a separation order against her husband on the ground of cruelty while they were still living together.

Now even at that early stage in my career I was not prepared to believe everything that my client told me

just because he was my client. For example, I was quite
prepared to believe that my client's denial of certain
acts of cruelty was false, but I did believe him when
he said that they were still living together. This allegation, if false, would have been so easy to disprove and I
could not think that anyone would be stupid enough to
make it, if it were not true. I travelled down to the
Court with my solicitor client and the husband, and to
be on the safe side I questioned him about his statement. As as result I was completely convinced that the
parties were living together. I thereupon told the
husband and the solicitor that I was glad to say that
we were bound to win the case. When asked for an
explanation I told them what was stated in *Stone's
Justices Manual*. 'But,' said the husband, 'my wife
has got a lawyer. Doesn't he know that?' 'He ought
to,' I said, 'but you know, Mr so-and-so, some lawyers
think they know, others look it up, and fortunately—
it's no credit to me of course—I am simply doing what
I was told to do—but I did look it up.' 'Well this
is fine,' said the husband, 'I'm almost sorry for the poor
girl. Here she is paying her good money to have lawyers'
(this was in the days before legal aid) 'and she is bound
to lose. Lucky I had you for my counsel.' 'Oh well,' I
said : 'I expect the solicitor for your wife was very busy.'

So we arrived at the Court in a very happy frame of
mind and I went in and took my seat. I noticed that
the clerk had a copy of *Stone's Justices Manual* in front
of him and I asked him if I could look at it. I did this
because I noticed that his edition was dated one year
later than mine. He lent it to me, and I was horrified to
find that during the year which had elapsed between
the two editions, the law had been changed, and that a
wife could get a separation order from her husband on

the ground of cruelty even if they were still living together. In other words after many years a monstrous
injustice to wives had been remedied. I had no time to
tell my client the sad news before the case was called
on. At any rate I didn't make a fool of myself in public
by taking a false point. I fought the case as best I could
and duly lost it. When it was all over, I met the husband outside the Court and explained what had happened. I said I was very sorry. I thought he was rather
nice about it, for all he said was this : 'That's all right,
son, but next time, son, do me a favour and get the
latest edition.'

So you must not only look it up but see that you look
it up in the latest case or the latest statute. Don't just
be satisfied with finding one thing in your favour. Make
certain that it hasn't been overruled either in another
case or by another Act of Parliament.

The next rule is : take a really good note in court.
Don't just sit back and listen. It is quite easy to get into
the habit of taking a good note and it will stand you
in good stead when you do. It will be very useful to
your master to have a pupil who always takes down a
full and reliable note. Reliability is the keynote. Write
down what the witness said—not just the favourable
part from your client's point of view. You must write
quickly and sufficiently legibly to be able to read it
yourself. If your master can read it as well, so much
the better, but that is not absolutely essential—speed,
accuracy, completeness and legibility-to-you—are the
essentials. There is an obvious advantage in learning
shorthand. The disadvantages are that it is certain that
no one else will be able to read it and that you yourself
may have more difficulty in cross-examining from a
shorthand than from a longhand note. There are, how-

Pupils
or
'Listen to this one'

ever, a few barristers who find the obvious advantage greater than the disadvantages.

As you get more experienced you will be able to anticipate a witness' answers and get them down in advance. But don't forget to alter the answer if your guess was wrong. It is quite a good tip to get down everything the judge takes down in the language he uses. Sometimes a judge reads out what he is writing. See that you take that down in the same language. Later on this may occur :

YOUR MASTER : My Lord, I'm sure the witness said that.

COUNSEL ON THE OTHER SIDE : My recollection is that he said just the opposite, my Lord.

YOUR MASTER : My learned pupil has a note, my Lord—(reading with difficulty)—Just after the part about the accident, my Lord. 'I left the money in a box by the bed. It was unlocked.'

JUDGE : Just one moment. Ah—yes—I have it. 'I left the money in a box by the bed. It was unlocked.' Yes—that's right, Mr Pringle. Thank you.

And you feel very pleased. And if you do that sufficiently often your master knows that he can rely on you.

Whether you can rely on him is another matter which will be touched on in a moment.

Your next rule is to write useful notes on law. It may be some time before you can do this. But you must try from the start. Whenever a point of law is involved look it up, preferably in the Bar Library, and write a note on it. Don't be satisfied until you have looked into every case and text book that can have a bearing on it. The librarians will be most helpful to you. The cases in the Bar Library are very well noted up and your researches will sometimes lead you to look up very many cases which have nothing to do with the subject. But don't be discouraged. You will eventually learn how to exclude irrelevant cases. But that only comes from experience.

If you follow these rules throughout your pupillage and you have the ability, you will have a very reasonable chance of being asked to stay on in the same chambers after your pupillage. And, if the chambers are busy chambers, you will be bound to succeed, if you have the necessary qualities already referred to. You will not need luck or influence. You will acquire a practice automatically.

Nearly every pupil regards his master as almost infallible, at any rate at the beginning of his pupillage. But, of course, he isn't. And, as time goes on, you should notice his mistakes and profit by them. If you have been unlucky and he is only very second-rate, you will have endless opportunities of doing this. Even if he is able, he will no doubt have his weaknesses. He may be good in court but weak on paper or vice versa. To begin with, you are almost bound to think he is good on paper. Drafting pleadings is from your point of view so technical that you are almost bound to admire anyone who can do that part of the work at all. But there are in fact very few barristers on the Common Law side whose pleadings are consistently first-rate. And pleadings are very important.

You may ask why in these modern times technical legal documents are necessary. Well, of course, they shouldn't be. No technicalities should be necessary. Just let the judge do what is right. But in a state where that could be done successfully there would be no necessity for any law at all. Moreover, if everything were left to the judge to do what is right, no one would know what the law was until the judge told them. Even if he were a perfect judge it would be rather awkward for people. But, of course, he would not be perfect.

So cases have to be decided either in accordance with Acts of Parliament or with previously decided cases. And the way in which a case has to be presented must be provided for. There must be rules of procedure. They are far from perfect. From time to time they are improved. Occasionally there is a step backwards.

In an imperfect world there will always have to be rules, however imperfect. And, for example, unless the plaintiff puts down in writing what his case is, the defendant will not know what case he has to meet. And, unless the defendant puts his case in writing, the plaintiff won't know how to meet the defence. And, once they have to be put in writing, there must be some rules as to how that is to be done. And these are the rules you have got to know. Unless you happen to be a pupil of one of the very few first-class draftsmen, the time will come when you should be able to spot mistakes in your master's pleadings.

It may be that, unless the rules are changed, your master will let you devil for him in court. Devilling is an unsatisfactory procedure, but it is difficult to see how it can be avoided. No one can be in two places at once. A barrister normally accepts instructions in a case long before there can be any question of it coming on for trial, and, as nine cases out of ten are settled long before trial, he could not carry on a practice at all if he refused to accept more than one case at a time. When he accepts the instructions in the first instance he has no idea whether or when it will come on for trial. So a busy barrister has to have help and, provided he employs devils of ability and experience, little or no harm is done.

But the employment of pupils is quite another matter. You are quite unfitted as a pupil to conduct any part of a case in court at all. It is an admirable (though terrifying) experience for you if you are called on to do so, but it is very bad luck on the client. It happened to Roger Thursby in *Brothers in Law*[1] on his first day as a pupil (this was before the six-months rule), and he didn't even know which side he was on. That was not an exaggeration, but, if he *had* known which side he was on, he would not at that stage in his career have been any more use to his unfortunate client. I did once start to open a case for the plaintiff in a County Court when I was devilling for counsel who had been briefed for the defendant.

There is nothing you can do about this practice of allowing pupils to devil except to profit by it as long as it exists. You will have the most horrifying experiences and, unless you are unusually phlegmatic, you will feel very much as a soldier going into action feels when you see your master's clerk making urgent signs to him that his presence is required elsewhere. 'Just tell him the tale, my dear fellow,' your master may say to you, 'just tell him the tale.' It is to be hoped you will have some idea of the tale. But for all the help you may receive from judges you will have terribly embarrassing moments, and, unless you are constitutionally incapable of blushing, you must be prepared to see a very red face in the looking-glass in the robing-room, if you're bold enough to look.

[1] Published by Michael Joseph Ltd. 1955; film first shown 1957.

But the advantage to you is tremendous. Having spluttered nonsense for your master before various judges, you will eventually have a simple little case which you can really understand how to conduct. And your client in the case will reap the benefit of the fact that you are not hearing your own voice in court for the first time. You will be much less frightened and will really be able to concentrate on doing the case. All the same, you will probably lose it if it is in the County Court and you have a much more experienced and able opponent, though this is less the case today than it was.

You may ask why the practice of pupils devilling is objectionable. Every surgeon, you will say, has to have his first cut. True enough. But before he was allowed that first cut he had watched many surgeons making many similar cuts and he may even have assisted in a minor way at such an operation. On the day you are qualified as a barrister you have probably never seen the outside of a brief, let alone the inside. And, if you have seen the inside of a court, it was either as an interested spectator or because you left your car too long somewhere. One year's experience of seeing barristers cut out legal appendices is surely short enough. It may be that medical students are allowed to do too many things to the public before they are qualified, but at least there is a good deal of control over them and they are not licensed to kill.

As soon as you have been a pupil for six months you are as licensed as any doctor, and if you win any cases in your first year it will be Providence and not you who secures a verdict for your client—or possibly even the justice of his case. But that will by no means necessarily follow if you are in charge of it.

8 *Barrister's Clerk*

In a sense the clerk is the most important person in chambers. If you get on the wrong side of the clerk at an early stage, there will be little hope for you in that set of chambers. In a good set of chambers the clerk is a friend to everyone in those chambers, and there exists a relationship and confidence between the members and their clerk which probably does not exist in any other profession.

Barristers' clerks are a race apart and the relationship between a barrister and his clerk is like no other. He probably starts as a boy in the Temple, running about doing anything that is required of him. But, just as you can show your master that you can be of use to him, so a boy can quickly show that he can be of use in chambers. If he sticks at it, he becomes a junior clerk and eventually, with luck, a clerk to a set of chambers.

That is a most enviable position if it is a flourishing set of chambers. He is paid mainly by commission, which is now 5 per cent, but he is also free to make arrangements with the barristers in his chambers for additional remuneration. This may take the form of a nominal salary or a small additional percentage on the fees. Often the clerk pays junior clerks the whole or part of their salaries. A clerk in busy chambers may easily earn altogether £3,000 or £4,000 per year or more.

Some clerks know the legal executives in solicitors'

offices very well and can influence the sending of briefs to members of the chambers. In this way a clerk can do a great deal for an able barrister. But he can do nothing for those of little ability except to give them the opportunity of showing their lack of skill in the first instance, and later, more as a matter of charity, directing to them cases which no one could lose or no one could win. A clerk will not normally recommend a barrister whom he does not consider fit to do the job. But he is a very good salesman when he thinks his products are of a high order.

Apart from his influence in obtaining actual work for the chambers the clerk's most important duties are in arranging the fees, keeping the books, and trying to prevent cases clashing or making suitable devilling arrangements if they do.

In your early days the clerk's word is pretty well law to you. Later on, if you succeed, your relationship will develop into a happy and understanding association.

A clerk in a good set of chambers has an assured position and a very substantial income and he has acquired both without any training whatever except that of experience. Until the last ten years or so some unsuccessful but still struggling barristers, who had had hundreds of pounds spent on their education, must have compared their position with that of their clerk rather ruefully. Perhaps some of them pondered whether it would not have been better if they had started as boys in the Temple.

Barristers never discuss fees with solicitors, or only in the rarest circumstances. There may have been an almost acrimonious discussion between the clerk and the solicitor on the subject—but the barrister knows nothing of this officially. For example :

Barrister and Clerk
or
'I've promised that opinion for Monday'

BARRISTER'S CLERK (on telephone): Hullo, Arthur. How much should I mark Mr Granite's brief in Toddle and Reindeer Cleaning?

SOLICITOR'S MANAGING CLERK: What d'you suggest?

BARRISTER'S CLERK: It's worth at least a couple of hundred, I should say.

SOLICITOR'S MANAGING CLERK: Here, careful—my heart's not as good as it was. I was thinking about fifty.

BARRISTER'S CLERK: Well you'd better think again. Fifty!

SOLICITOR'S MANAGING CLERK: Don't make me laugh, Albert. Leave out the funny bits and tell me what you do want.

BARRISTER'S CLERK: I've told you—two hundred.

SOLICITOR'S MANAGING CLERK: I heard you the first time. I thought that was a music-hall turn. Make it seventy-five.

BARRISTER'S CLERK: Look, old man, I wouldn't ask anyone in the chambers to do it for that—I tell you what though, as it's you I'll make it a hundred and fifty.

SOLICITOR'S MANAGING CLERK: A hundred.

BARRISTER'S CLERK: Can't be done, old boy.

SOLICITOR'S MANAGING CLERK: Well—a hundred and twenty-five.

BARRISTER'S CLERK: Terribly sorry, old boy, it's just not on. I shall probably have to return a couple of briefs for it.

SOLICITOR'S MANAGING CLERK: Well, I'll have to ask my principal about it. He'll bark like a dog.

BARRISTER'S CLERK: Give him a biscuit then.

SOLICITOR'S MANAGING CLERK: Hold on—(pause) . . .

SOLICITOR: Good afternoon, Mr Bilsby. I understand

you are asking a hundred and fifty in the Reindeer Cleaning?

BARRISTER'S CLERK : That's right, sir.

SOLICITOR : Well, it's ridiculous. I could get anyone in the Temple to do it for less. There are others, you know.

BARRISTER'S CLERK : There's only one Mr Granite, sir. I'm very sorry, sir, I couldn't ask him to do it for less. It ought to be two hundred.

SOLICITOR : It's highway robbery. We send your chambers a lot of work, you know.

BARRISTER'S CLERK : I know you do, sir, and that's why I knocked it down to a hundred and fifty. I wouldn't have done that for many people.

SOLICITOR : Mr Granite will be there all the time?

BARRISTER'S CLERK : Now, sir—you know me, sir. Have we ever let you down?

SOLICITOR : Well you'll be letting me down unless I can tell my clients that you'll do it for less than a hundred and fifty.

BARRISTER'S CLERK : I'm terriby sorry, sir.

SOLICITOR : And what about refreshers? It'll take three or four days.

BARRISTER'S CLERK : I thought of seventy-five.

SOLICITOR : Really! That's half the brief fee. Look, I'll tell you what—I'll agree to one hundred and fifty if you'll keep the refreshers to thirty. My clients aren't made of money, you know.

BARRISTER'S CLERK : I'll make them forty-five, sir. I couldn't do less—that's below a third of the brief fee.

SOLICITOR : Very well, then—but I think it's too bad not meeting us more.

Three hours later.

SOLICITOR : Oh—how are you, Mr Granite? It's very

good of you to do this thing for us. Your clerk tells me you have had to return two other cases.

BARRISTER : Have I? I leave it all to Albert. Very glad I can do it for you.

SOLICITOR : I'm not flattering you, but I wouldn't have anyone else in the Temple to do this case.

9 *Second Year*

I HAVE already indicated that in Common Law and Criminal chambers a barrister's chances of success are infinitely greater than they were and, provided he gets into good chambers, he can look forward with confidence to making a reasonable income from the moment his pupillage finishes. Nevertheless I think it may be of interest to set out in the original language what I wrote in 1958 about the barrister's second year. Here it is.

When you have finished your pupillage the struggle begins. If you are lucky and stay on in busy chambers or, better still, with your budding Lord Chancellor, all you need to do is to work hard and, if you are good enough, your success will be automatic. But if you are less fortunate and have to take what you can get, the struggle will be a hard one. Then you must be sure that you miss no opportunity that may come your way. Above all, you must arrive early and stay in chambers late in the hope that something will happen. If you get dispirited and keep short hours, you may miss a chance that will not be repeated. You must try to get as much devilling as possible and persuade your clerk to let it be known in other chambers that you are available when wanted.

In this way you may gradually acquire a practice of your own. But you must not allow the many disappointments to discourage you. The time may come when you devil for other barristers in County Courts and Magistrates' Courts. You will read a case thoroughly and feel quite confident that you can do it well. You will be waiting poised like a runner at the start, when the man for whom you have devilled will come in, puffing hard : 'Just made it, my dear chap,' he will say, as the case is called on. The next moment he is opening the case to the judge and you think that all your work has been wasted. Never mind. Think yourself lucky you had the opportunity, and learn what you can by the way the case is fought. You were ready to do it yourself. Consider how you would have done it. Spot any mistakes that are made or that you would have made. And once again, if anything happens for which you don't know chapter and verse, look it up.

Another time you may be luckier—to begin with anyway. You go down to the Court on behalf of someone who doesn't turn up in time. Or perhaps he turns up just as you have lost it. It was a case that couldn't have been lost but somehow or other you managed to lose it. The judge brushed your submissions aside and, when you quoted something out of a text book to him, said, with a not unkindly smile :

'I think that case is rather different, Mr Green.'

'But I submit, your Honour——' you persist.

'I know you do, Mr Green,' says the judge, still pleasantly, 'but I'm against you.'

One thing you must always do, and cases have often been lost as a result of a failure to do it. Always take with you any authorities which may be necessary to support your case. Never assume that the judge knows them. He may or may not. Fill up your bag with them. Take two bags, if necessary. The exercise will do you no harm. If you are bashful about bringing into Court eighteen volumes of law reports when you are fighting a claim for £17 before the Registrar, by all means leave them in the robing-room in the first instance; but don't hesitate to send for them or fetch them yourself if you need them or any of them. It may well be that nine times out of ten you won't need them. But don't let that make you leave them behind on the tenth time. Let nothing discourage you. A case in a County Court many years ago involved a dispute between landlord and tenant, and counsel on both sides took with them vast numbers of authorities and argued the case for four days. The judge listened most politely and allowed case after case to be quoted to him. At the end he reserved judgment. After some little time his judgment was delivered :

'The plaintiff,' he said, 'swore that the paint on oil paintings ran. She was positive about it. Oil paintings cannot run. I therefore reject the evidence of the plaintiff and there will be judgment for the defendant.'

The judgment was, of course, a little longer than that, but that was the substance of it. Not a single case was referred to. Counsel on each side might have saved himself a lot of trouble. In point of fact, the books were a great help to one of them. He had gone to Court in a small car with the books—about thirty of them— in the dickey. A back tyre burst and the car would have overturned but for the weight of the books. Moral : you never know.

Accept nothing just because someone says it. There are always misapprehensions as to the law going around—sometimes for many years. Experienced barristers are not infallible, nor are judges. Seek to understand the principle behind every decision. That is the important part of it.

Always find something to do until your practice has

begun to exist and then to increase and finally to reach
a stage when you need a holiday.

If, in spite of your seeking every opportunity to help
other people either in court or by looking up points of
law for them, you cannot keep yourself busy, don't
mope or read novels. Stay in chambers and find something to do. You may find it possible to write articles
for newspapers and magazines on simple legal problems.
At least you can try. Or you can try your hand at
writing articles on important and difficult points of
law which arise, and sending them to legal magazines.
No harm will be done if they're not taken. You will
have kept yourself busy and learned something. Alternatively, chase up some point of law or practice which
you're not sure about. There are plenty of them.

Some suggestions are set out in the Appendix but
any good lawyer will tell you some more.

I have set out this chapter in its original form because
I think the advice is sound, although the facts are somewhat out of date. Your briefs are likely to come in
much sooner and in far larger quantities than they did
for the young people for whom this book was written
in 1958. But it's to be hoped that you will still have
time to learn. The best people in all professions are
learning all the time. And the standard at the Bar will
swiftly deteriorate unless the new rising generation of
barristers tries to learn as much as it can of the ins and
outs of their profession. If you are prepared to sit back
and to accept complacently the briefs which come to
you, not because of your own ability but because of the
amount of crime and legal aid and the shortage of
barristers, you will never do the job really well. It is
true that for the reasons which I have mentioned you

Barrister in Chambers
or
Where will the next one come from?

may obtain a large income and have as many briefs as you can manage, you may even become a judge, but you will never have the satisfaction which comes from doing a job to the best of your ability. Moreover, if there should be a recession in crime or legal aid or if competition at the Bar becomes greater, you may start to find your practice slipping away from you. It is also very important, not only from your own point of view but from the point of view of your profession that you should at all times seek to maintain the highest standard of which you are capable.

10 *Life at the Bar*

THERE may be twenty or more or (rarely) only two
or three barristers in a set of chambers. The head of
the chambers is the tenant, and is usually the senior
barrister. (If there is a Q.C. in chambers he is usually
the head.) He pays the rent and rates to the Inn where
the chambers are situated and is in turn paid a rent
by the other members of the chambers. The amount
which he will receive from the other members of the
chambers will, of course, vary with what space they
occupy. If you have a large room all to yourself you
will naturally pay more than if you share a room
with two others or have a very small room to
yourself. Your rent to the tenant covers all the
facilities provided by the chambers, except the services
of the senior clerk. His remuneration was stated in
Chapter 8.

In return for your rent and the remuneration which
you pay the clerk you will have full use of the chambers'
library and the services of the junior clerk or clerks and
typists. If there is a shorthand typist it is unlikely that
in the early stages you will have any use for her or be
allowed any. The head of the chambers decides how
the chambers should be run but he often consults the
senior members. As I have said, the Bar is a happy profession and the atmosphere in most sets of chambers is a
happy one. Every one is always ready to help you and
people are not quick to rely on their strict legal rights—
as to notice or the like. The rent which you are likely

to have to pay upon entering chambers will vary from £200 to £350. What you pay your clerk will partly depend upon the extent of your practice. You will probably pay him between 5 per cent and 10 per cent of your fees and it is possible that you will also pay him a small salary as well. Later on you may have better accommodation and pay a higher rent. You may even employ a full time shorthand-typist or secretary of your own.

In addition, unless you are in the Chancery Division, you will join a circuit. The cost of this is small and varies according to the circuit. On the South Eastern circuit it consists of an annual subscription of £8. If you have influence in one of the big towns such as Liverpool, Manchester, Leeds, Birmingham, Swansea or Bristol you will probably join local chambers there. Life will be very much the same there, except that there are, of course, fewer barristers and there is no Temple or Lincoln's Inn to house them. The chambers are dotted about the town.

If you practise in London you may in addition to joining a circuit join the Bar Mess of one or more of the Courts of the Crown Court which used to be called Quarter Sessions.

Whether or not you acquire a circuit practice at the expense of working in London is a matter which you have to decide, but if you start to get work on circuit, you should take advice about the future from someone of experience.

To join a circuit you must normally apply within a year of your being called to the Bar. If you practise in London, whether you ever go on circuit will depend chiefly on whether there is work of that kind in your chambers, and of course whether you know any

The Bear Garden
or
How much of it is really necessary?

solicitors in the country who want to brief you at the local Crown Court.

You should normally get to your chambers about 9.30 and leave about 6 or 6.30 p.m. That is only a general statement. Some barristers arrive extremely early or leave equally late. You will not normally go to chambers on Saturdays.

Legal holidays (i.e. when the High Court is not sitting) are long. Two months in the Summer (August and September), about three weeks at Christmas and about ten days at Easter and at Whitsun. But you won't take holidays of that length, or anything like it. There is work to be done in all the vacations, and you may always pick up a brief in County Courts, the Crown Court or Magistrates' Courts because a colleague is away. There is also some work done in the High Court. If you are wise, in your first years in chambers, including your pupillage year, you will cut down your holidays to the minimum necessary for your health and to prevent your getting stale. Later on, when you become really busy, then you will have to insist on taking long holidays—not the full length legal holidays but, say, at least a month in the Summer and a week at Christmas, Easter and Whitsun. Most busy juniors need that amount of rest. The junior Bar, at the top, is probably the hardest-worked profession in the world.

I have already indicated that Legal Aid has been of great benefit to the Bar as well as to the public. Pretty well every barrister has his name on the roll of counsel who are prepared to do work under the Legal Aid and Advice Act. In the old days before the Legal Aid and Advice Act, the amount paid to counsel doing work of this kind was either purely nominal or nothing at all.

The situation is very different now. Proper fees are arranged on all briefs delivered under the Legal Aid and Advice Act, and in the Criminal Courts and County Courts these fees are paid in full. In the High Court they are reduced by 10 per cent. In Common Law chambers probably 30 per cent to 40 per cent of the work done by the members of chambers is done under the Legal Aid and Advice Act. In criminal chambers the percentage is probably more like 80 per cent or 90 per cent.

In your earlier days you may be asked to devil cases for other barristers. When you first start to do this you may not be paid anything. Normally if a devil does a case for someone else he is paid half the fee. But the experience and the chance of being heard in court are worth far more to him than the fee.

So, whatever you do, don't turn up your nose at unpaid devilling. The person to be sorry for is your lay client, not you. Devilling ought never to be unpaid, because only experienced and competent people should be employed to devil. Fortunately for you this is not always the case.

But, when you succeed at the Bar, always pay your devils.

Lunch is a hurried meal during term time. You will either have it in your Inn, in the Law Courts or in one of the cafés near the Law Courts. A busy junior often has only a few minutes for it. When the Court adjourns at lunch time he may have to attend an application before the Master in Chambers and, by the time that is over, he may have to be back in Court again. In addition he may have to have an urgent conference in the case which he is conducting.

Advice is easy to obtain in chambers, and some of it

may be very good. Nearly all of it is useful. The important thing to remember in asking advice is that the person whom you are asking has not looked up the point. So look it up yourself first and then draw the attention of the person you are asking to what you have found. For example, if you ask advice about a County Court case from a senior member of chambers, who no longer goes to the County Court, he may well have forgotten the rules there, or they may have changed since he practised in those courts. So, if it's a question of practice, have the rule ready for him to look at.

You will soon adopt the normal method of talking about cases, which is to identify yourself with the lay client. 'I am a dentist who pulled out the wrong tooth, etc.' 'I am a lady travelling in an underground train. A complete stranger says to me——' and so on.

One of the things you will get practice in is listening to people without interrupting. The second-rate practitioner from time to time interrupts the judge, and sometimes you get the undignified spectacle of the judge and counsel talking to each other at the same time, and neither hearing what the other has to say. It is only a question of self-control. There is sure to be at least one talkative member of your chambers. Practise listening to him without interrupting till he really has finished. But you must *listen* to him too or there is no point in the exercise. Deliberately cultivate the ability to keep your mouth shut until it is plain that the other person has finished. The best advocate keeps absolutely quiet until the judge has finished, even if the judge has interrupted him. He may look hard at the judge at the same time, but he keeps quiet. Many years ago, long before the war, things went a bit wrong in the Court of Appeal and a puisne judge who happened to be sitting there was heard to say quite loudly to one of his brethren: 'Oh, do let me finish.' But that sort of thing happens once in a century.

11 *Behaviour in Court*

WHAT you say in Court is important but an increasing number of advocates do not seem to realise that how you say it is important too. It is not necessary to have professional elocution or deportment lessons but many young men would find that their earlier cases would go more happily if they deliberately considered how to make a good impression from the moment they stood up. It is odd that, in a profession where the voice has constantly to be used, few practitioners trouble to acquire any facility in using it, except by accident.

The first rule is never to speak while the judge is speaking to you and practically never while your opponent is speaking. Occasionally it may be necessary to interrupt your opponent but it is rare that this need be done in the middle of a sentence. Next, open your mouth wide and speak clearly and deliberately and not too fast. Take the trouble to let your sentences have a beginning, a middle and an end. The judge may interrupt you in the middle of a sentence sometimes (he shouldn't, but it will happen from time to time) but do not rely on this to justify the use of sloppy language.

Of course, few of you will at first be able to make polished speeches. But that will only come with experience if you realise the necessity for it at the start. At the one end of the scale are the Crabtrees, who ought never to have come to the Bar. But between them and the first-rate advocate, there are many who do not bother either about their language or the voice in which it is spoken. See that you bother about both. Few masters tell their pupils anything about this.

What is required is only self-discipline. You must make yourself speak clearly and intelligibly from the start, until it is your second nature. Look at the judge or the witness when you address him; don't mumble into your waistcoat, and don't drop your voice at the end of a sentence.

Try to avoid parentheses in the normal way. You will find them a source of embarrassment to you at the beginning. When you are more experienced you may find a swift parenthesis effective.

'And now, my Lord. I will deal with the evidence of the plaintiff. Your Lordship will remember that he said—just before he asked for a glass of water—that etc. etc.'

But not:

'Now, my Lord, I will come to the evidence of the plaintiff. But before I come to his evidence I would just like to remind your Lordship of the case which we came here to meet.'

Well, if you want to tell his Lordship about that, say so first.

'Before I come to the evidence of the plaintiff I should like to remind your Lordship etc.'

So speak up and speak simply. Good notes may be a great help to you. If you have a note on the desk in front of you with each subject (on which you want to address the judge or examine or cross-examine the witness) clearly on it, you will not be worrying whether you may forget to make a point or ask a question. But they must be written very clearly and in very few words. You may never have to refer to them, but most advocates find the practice invaluable. Such notes are not simply an assurance that nothing will be omitted, but they give the advocate the opportunity of concentrating entirely on what he is saying. Such an advocate will never be harassed suddenly by the thought, 'Now what was that question I thought of last night?'—while he is busy suggesting to the witness that his evidence is inconsistent with the letter on page 38 of the correspondence. Although you will in due course adopt your own method of preparing a case, you will probably find it an advantage to start by conducting your case from your own notes rather than from the brief itself.

The actual stance in Court is also of importance. This does not mean that you have to stand to attention or be uncomfortable. But it does mean that you should not get into habits which may annoy a judge.

'Do stop swaying from side to side,' a judge has been heard to say to counsel. It must not be thought that, if counsel for the plaintiff sways from side to side, the judge is going to decide the case in favour of the defendant. Of course not. But if you irritate the judge he may say something to you which puts *you* off your stroke. And if *you* get rattled, you may make a mess of the case.

That is the point of all this advice. Judges are human, but they do want to decide cases correctly, however badly they may be presented. But if you present a case badly and your opponent presents it well, there is always the chance that the judge may make a mistake.

If you have a stormy passage because the judge can't hear what you say, doesn't like you exposing a vast expanse of shirt, objects to the way you push your wig almost off your head, you may very well in your embarrassment leave out an essential point or put it in such

A court at the Old Bailey
or
'Members of the jury, you cannot convict my client' (*can't they!*)

a muddled form that the judge never really understands it. And it is a vital rule of advocacy that you must ensure that the judge understands the point which you are making. Advocates do not like too talkative judges, but they do not like too silent ones either, because with them it is sometimes impossible to tell whether they have appreciated the point or not. And it is a little annoying when, having put your point with the judge saying nothing at all, you eventually say :

'I hope your Lordship has followed my submission,' and complete silence continues. That is far less likely to happen today than some years ago.

You will, however, find that silence is one of the most effective weapons that a judge can use. Silence sometimes combined, in the lesser judges, with a look at the witness which implies 'So that's what you say, is it?' and which, in the case of the worst judges, is actually followed by that expression.

Don't wear extravagant or unusual dress in Court or chambers. Follow the normal fashion whatever it may be. It is quite true that, if you succeed, some piece of foppishness or vanity affecting your clothes may even be to your advantage, but in your early days it would only do you harm. Dress decently and wear your robes properly. For example, don't allow your bands to hang round your ear, and see that they conceal the stud and are clean and well pressed.

One of the mistakes which too many advocates make is to proffer their opinion to the Court. You are not allowed to do this. It is your business to make submissions to the Court. Your own opinion is irrelevant. This is, in fact, lucky for you. Because, if you were permitted to give your opinion, you would never be able to represent your client in a case where you thought he was in the wrong. It wouldn't be much use starting off with :

'My Lord, in this case I appear for the plaintiff who, in my opinion, has no cause of action.'

Your opinion might, of course, be wrong (consider what Dr Johnson said about this : page 151), but your case would hardly start off in a very auspicious way with that opening. And, if you have appreciated the advice given on integrity, you will understand that you could not possibly say to the judge that you thought your client was in the right, if in fact you thought he was in the wrong.

Unfortunately that is what a number of advocates do. They do not, of course, intend to deceive the Court or appreciate what they are doing, but they use the words 'I think' or 'in my opinion' as though they were synonymous with 'in my submission.' No top class advocate ever makes this mistake and you can recognise the inferior (or inexperienced or untaught) brand when you hear it made.

On one occasion a County Court judge was considering a difficult point of law. Appearing before him was an advocate of great experience in the particular branch of law concerned. 'I wish I could ask you what you really thought,' said the judge.

See that you never tell the judge 'what you really think'—except out of Court, if you know him well enough to do so.

Remember that you have a duty to the Court as well as to your client. Apart from your duty never to mislead a judge, it may be your duty to disclose to a judge matters which are against your client's interests. In an undefended divorce, for example, if there is evidence of collusion you must let the judge know about it. Judges trust counsel and will often say, for example, if you hand up to them a large bundle of correspondence in an undefended divorce: 'Are there any particular letters which you think I ought to read?' And if counsel only refers in his reply to two letters, the judge will probably not look at any of the others. The normal rule is: if you are not sure whether something should be disclosed or not, disclose it. In exceptional cases seek advice from someone of experience, if you have the opportunity.

12 *Behaviour out of Court*

THERE is nothing unprofessional in appearing for a lay client who is a friend, but on the whole it is not a desirable practice. It is especially undesirable in more serious cases, because your friendship might lead you into an excess of enthusiasm for your case. This in turn might lead to your doing things which you should not do. Although an advocate may throw himself heart and soul into his case, he ought to be able to take a completely detached view of the actual result. It is, of course, true that in your early days winning a case may be very important to you personally and it is therefore difficult for you to take this detached view. But you should, as far as possible, aim at detachment. This is simply because too much bias in favour of your client, too much identification of yourself with the case, may lead you in the heat of battle into unsatisfactory practices. To take an extreme case, it would be difficult for a devoted husband to defend his wife, on a charge of murder, with detachment. And if, in such a case, he could by improperly manipulating the evidence help to secure her acquittal, would he be proof against such temptation? How many devoted husbands would be?

This is not intended to imply that in no case should you act for a friend in Court, but, before you do so, you ought to consider the nature of the case and to bear in mind the high standard of integrity required of you when you decide whether it will be satisfactory for you to appear.

In no circumstances should you appear where it is conceivable that you may have been a witness to some part of the transaction leading up to the litigation. Many years ago a famous advocate, whose enthusiasm sometimes outran his sense of propriety, offended against this rule. In consequence, during his cross-examination of a witness the answers from time to time were like this : 'No, that was the occasion when *you* said to me that etc. etc.' The great advocate did not appear to be embarrassed, but he ought to have been.

There is no objection whatever to your being briefed by solicitors who are friends of yours. It is they who ought to consider whether it is really in the interests of their clients to brief you. But you must not let your friendship with a solicitor lead you into improper practices, such as doing some of his work for him, i.e. interviewing a witness or having conferences at the solicitor's office. Except when no solicitor is employed (see p. 45) you must never interview your lay client in the absence of your solicitor or his representative. That is another reason why it may be unsatisfactory to appear for a close friend, because you must not discuss the case with him when you are alone together. Private telephone calls when the solicitor is not at one end of the line are equivalent to interviews and equally objectionable.

Don't go touting for work in any circumstances. There are all sorts of ways of doing this. Don't adopt any of them. If you are going to get on, you will get on without doing that kind of thing, and, if you are not going to get on, the little extra work you get will not either make you successful or counteract the bad impression which you will make on many people inside and outside the law.

A Gallery at the Law Courts
or
'It all depends on the judge really'

The bars and public houses in the vicinity of the Temple are visited regularly by solicitors' clerks and barristers' clerks. Never join these parties. There are a few perfectly reputable barristers who do on occasion go to one of these bars with a solicitor, but it is not a desirable practice. In the vicinity of the Temple the relationship between barrister and solicitor should, as far as possible, be entirely professional. What you do with your own friends, whether solicitors or not, when you are away from the Temple is entirely your own affair.

So, of course, is your general behaviour unconnected with your profession, but an objective bird's-eye view of the barrister in private life may perhaps be of use to you.

The public's ignorance of the law, combined with the drama with which it is associated, tend to make the barrister feel rather important.

'Are you a barrister? What does it feel like to do a murder case?' are questions which almost every barrister has been asked at some stage. In consequence, you are likely, if you are not careful, to form rather too high an opinion of yourself from an early stage. And, as you get more experience and are able to tell legal stories of absorbing interest, that opinion is not likely to lessen. It is always possible, therefore, that you may become a crashing bore. So watch it. Moreover it is important to remember that many things which you learn in a case may have been confidential even though the matter has been fought in open court. You can never normally be compelled to divulge what your client has told you. Make sure that, for the pupose of a good story, you don't voluntarily tell your friends and acquaintances about it. It will sometimes be a temptation to do so. This applies equally of course to your own and your master's cases. In other words, never abuse the confidence which is given to you, even though it may flatter your conceit to do so.

They were discussing appeals to the House of Lords in Hall. 'I've been four times to the House of Lords,' said the late X.Y.Z. 'Each time I was for the appellant and each time I won.'

'Really,' said A.B.C. 'I've only been once. I was for the respondent and I lost.'

X.Y.Z. was not deflated, although he was an unsuccessful hack of a barrister, in his later years picking up most of his cases by impressing (Heaven knows how) his fellow members at golf clubs. A.B.C. on the other hand was one of the most brilliant and successful members of the Bar.

Don't become like X.Y.Z. either in Hall or on the golf course.

13 *The Solicitor*

IF you are at the Common Law Bar and you meet a solicitor socially he will in all probability say: 'We do mostly Chancery work,' or, if that is too blatant an untruth: 'I don't deal with the litigation side in our office.'

Many solicitors, on meeting a barrister, think it incumbent on themselves to offer an immediate excuse for not sending him work. Alternatively, they may talk expansively of the briefs they might send him—and not send them.

'That's really very interesting, Mr Green. We're looking for someone who'll take our small work in the County Court. Our man's getting too big for it.'

You murmur something about its being very kind of him or its being very nice or you just give a sort of cough and go a bit red in the face.

'Let me see—where are your chambers?' This certainly looks like business. You answer that question immediately and with accuracy—and at dictation speed.

'As a matter of fact we've got a small thing at Ilford next Wednesday. I'm not sure if my clerk's briefed anyone yet. D'you happen to be free? But, of course, you wouldn't know without your clerk.'

Wouldn't you? You're almost perpetually free. But it wouldn't do to say so too obviously. On the other hand, you don't want to misrepresent your practice to him.

'I think I am, as a matter of fact,' you say. (Those five words 'as a matter of fact' serve many useful purposes. They are not infrequently used when it is *not* a matter of fact.)

'Splendid. Well—perhaps you'll get your clerk to give me a ring.'

Now you really are getting somewhere.

'Or better still—I'll ring him.'

Not better still at all. He never does ring. But you meet him six months later, and he hasn't forgotten. He slaps you on the back.

'Hullo—hullo—how are you? Taking silk yet? Sorry about that thing I mentioned to you, but my clerk had already briefed someone else. Pity. We lost it.'

You murmur something which you think is appropriate.

'That's all right, old boy. It won't break us exactly.' (Guffaws). 'I've had one or two other things since then, but I thought they'd be too small for you. Making quite a name for yourself—I expect—by now.'

'Oh—well——' you say modestly, being ready to take up that little matter with your conscience later.

'As a matter of fact,' proceeds your tormentor, 'it is a bit of luck our meeting today. I can pick your brains. You know all about landlord and tenant, I suppose?'

Conscience is now of no account. Expediency, on the other hand, calls for caution.

'Oh—well——' you say again.

'Well—it's like this. I've got a client—a nasty piece of work really—but that's another story—and he owns a lot of property down at . . . now, I can never remember the name of the place—never mind—somewhere in the South. Now this chap——'

He then proceeds to tell you a lengthy story involving

six different parties, four Acts of Parliament and three leading cases. You have heard of two of the Acts of Parliament and even read one or two of the sections (one Act contains 80 and the other 60 sections), you have a vague idea of the third and you're quite right in not recognising the fourth, as he's misquoted it. Finally he says :

'Now he hasn't a hope, has he?'

You pause for a moment. 'Oh, well'—seems inappropriate.

'Now don't be prejudiced by what I say. I want *your* opinion. Don't often get a chance like this—and no fee.' (Guffaws).

'Well,' you begin—and at that moment you are saved by your hostess.

'Now you two lawyers,' she says, 'break it up,' and she leads you away. Half-an-hour later you are with a beautiful blonde, talking about yourself at length and tediously (having first explained why you haven't done any murder cases) when you get a tap on your arm.

'Got to go now, dear boy. Look—I'll tell you what . . . I'll send the papers down to your chambers and you give me an opinion. Professionally, I mean. Shame to ask you at a party. Cheerio.' Six months later at a golf club he accosts you in the bar.

'Hullo, there. What a bit of luck. I've been wanting to explain to you about that case I never sent you.'

The odd thing about this type is that he always remembers exactly what particular story he's told you —and this in spite of the fact that he's told plenty of others to your colleagues.

'You know I said I never liked the fellow. Well— blow me down if he didn't go bankrupt the next day.

Barrister and Solicitors at a County Court
or
'I am sorry to have to ask you this question, madam'

Well—that put an end to that. I still think I was right. I know you weren't quite so sure. However, it doesn't matter now. Fortunately we'd had our costs right up to date.' (Guffaws).

Well, you'll never see him in your chambers, until perhaps many years later, when you're established as a successful junior.

For the most part in your early days you will meet the legal executives but, of course, from time to time you will meet the solicitor himself. You will normally find him understanding, helpful and reliable. But there are others. And your difficulty in your early days is to know which is which. It is very important to know. It has already been said that a brief sent to you by a solicitor may be absolutely reliable and it may be the reverse. A brief has been known to contain : 'The plaintiff is unable to give evidence as he is ill, but the evidence of the other witnesses should be sufficient to prove the case. P.S. The plaintiff is dead. It is believed that the other side are unaware of this, and counsel will no doubt do his best to cover this.'

That was a case where the cause of action died with the plaintiff.

Only experience and an unswerving determination to maintain your own integrity will enable you to deal with this aspect of your work, but, when in doubt, you should consult senior members of your chambers.

As you become more experienced and get to know your clients better you should encourage them to come to you at an early stage of an action. Quite a number of cases have been won wholly or in part by reason of the letters written before action. That does not mean that a false case succeeds because of the correspondence, but it does mean that a case, which ought in fact to succeed but might fail for lack of proof, does succeed because of the letters written in the early stages. Before drafting such letters it is important to be sure of your ground and there the solicitor is of vital consequence. Once you are committed to an unfounded allegation it can do incalculable harm. But conversely, if you set on record your case correctly at an early stage, it may be of great advantage to you. For example, if your client is making a serious allegation against some-one, say fraud, and you set out in a letter with great care the allegations of fraud and invite the proposed defendant to explain his conduct or alternatively to pay up, he will have to commit himself to an explana-tion at an early stage in the proceedings. It may well be that later on that explanation will not suit his case at all. Then it will be too late. But don't be led into making allegations against other people by a solicitor's instructions, without first assuring yourself that there is a reasonable possibility that the allegations are justified. Horrible things will happen to you if you don't take this advice to heart.

For example, when cross-examining a witness in the County Court your solicitor client may suddenly ask you to put to the witness that he has been convicted of a crime. Unless the information your solicitor has received and is passing on to you is correct the question will rebound on you with some force. In Chapter 25 on pages 184 to 187 I give an example of the way such a situation can sometimes be dealt with.

You are, as you are aware, solely dependent on your solicitor for paying you, and he is under no legal obligation to do so. Sometimes solicitors will not pay you at all and sometimes they will ask for a reduction of the fees. You must leave matters of this sort to your clerk. It is his province and he should know what to do in your best interests. You certainly don't. You may, of course, discuss such matters with your clerk, but don't dictate to him what to do. Most solicitors pay in full and without question, but there is a tendency on the part of less reputable firms to take advantage of younger men, whose clerks don't like to give offence by refusing work without payment in advance.

It is seldom worth making a complaint to the Law Society, though, if it is proved that a solicitor has been paid by his client, the Society will try to make him pay the barrister. There are exceptions to most rules but on the whole you should leave all questions of fees to your clerk and get on with your work.

14 *The Legal Executive or Managing Clerk*

I HAVE already said that the managing clerk of the old days has been almost entirely replaced by the legal executive. On the whole managing clerks were older and more experienced though less technically qualified than the legal executives. The following incident from the original edition is perhaps more likely to have taken place with a managing clerk than with a legal executive but on the whole I think it is worth keeping in this new edition. There is a moral, though I doubt if there are many Mr Trents around. I reproduce it in the language of the original edition.

Your clerk introduces you to Mr Truffle, the solicitor's managing clerk. He has been with his firm for many years and your clerk has persuaded him to let you do a small case for him. He is shown in to your room, which you probably share with one or two others, who may or may not go out when you have your conference.

'How d'you do, Mr Green?' says Mr Truffle. 'It's nice of you to do this little thing for us.' He knows quite well that, from the moment you were told the brief was coming to you, you have been waiting in suspense for it to arrive, but he speaks as though you were a very busy junior and were doing him a favour. But don't be misled by this act of kindness into giving yourself airs. If you did, you might even have the brief withdrawn from you on the spot. Mr Truffle enjoys crumbling his bread for you sparrows, but not if you misuse his hat. Mr Trent, for example, who was born with an over-weening self-confidence, would not normally be the man for Mr Truffle in the early stages. And most clerks, realising this, would keep Mr Truffle away from Mr Trent. Mr Trent would probably have started the conference like this :

'Ah—good morning, Mr Truffle. Please sit down. There's no trouble at all about this. I wonder if you fellows would mind leaving us. I want to talk to Mr Truffle privately.'

The fellows leave, and Mr Trent returns to Mr Truffle.

'It's about the brief, Mr Truffle,' he begins.

'Yes?' says Mr Truffle enquiringly.

'Yes,' continues Mr Trent, 'there are one or two things about it I'd like to get straight.'

'Such as?' queries Mr Truffle, still unaware of what is to come but sensing that it is something unusual.

'Yes, Mr Truffle. It's quite all right this time, but I thought it might help if I told you how I like my instructions to be drafted. It'll save us both trouble in the future.'

Mr Truffle breathes hard for the moment. He is not often at a loss for words. His failure to intervene at that early stage gives Mr Trent the chance to dig this particular grave deeper.

'In the first place,' he goes on, 'there's not really much point in giving me instructions which merely repeat the proofs of evidence. I had to read them in case there was anything else besides, but they might have been a carbon copy. Rather better if they had

A doorway in the Inner Temple
or
'Client of yours?'

been. Then I should have known. D'you see what I mean? Waste of your time and of mine.'

At this stage Mr Truffle is about to say that he is sorry to have wasted Mr Trent's time and, in the circumstances, he'll take the brief elsewhere, but he is still so shocked that the words do not come quickly enough. So Mr Trent goes on digging.

'Then another thing. You ask me to press for a special order as to costs. There's no power to grant it. Someone in your office should look these things up. If I hadn't done so, I might have made a fool of myself in court. I'm quite new to the game, you know, and most newly-called barristers accept what's in their instructions at their face value. They come some nasty croppers. However, it's all right fortunately this time.'

'Mr Trent,' begins Mr Truffle.

'No, please don't apologise,' goes on Mr Trent. 'It's the same with most solictors, I know. I don't suppose your office is any different from the others. So you needn't feel too badly about it. Of course there are a few firms whose instructions are really first class. But they are very much *rarae aves*—Latin, you know— rare birds.'

'Rare birds, did you say?' Mr Truffle gets in. 'I don't think I caught your name, sir?'

'Trent, Anthony Trent. Rather a good name for a barrister, don't you think?'

Mr Truffle murmurs something.

'I didn't quite catch,' says Mr Trent politely.

'I just said rare birds, Mr Trent, rare birds. But I said it in English. It was very good of you to translate it for me. We managing clerks are a pretty ignorant lot, you know.'

Mr Truffle has by this time recovered himself and he is beginning to enjoy Mr Trent. An account of the interview will go down extremely well in the bar at 'The Feathers.'

'It's not your fault,' says Mr Trent. 'The Education Act wasn't much use to you.'

'Alas, no, sir,' says Mr Truffle, 'alas no. We have to learn as we go along. That's why I'm so grateful to you, sir, for your help.'

'Don't mention it, please,' says Mr Trent. 'I would do the same for anyone.'

'Might I suggest,' says Mr Truffle, '—very humbly of course—that you choose your victims rather carefully.'

'Victims?' queries Mr Trent. 'Victims?'

'Victims of circumstances, Mr Trent,' says Mr Truffle.

Now Mr Truffle is no fool and, although at first he was going to withdraw the brief immediately, it suddenly dawns on him that a dose or two of Mr Trent would be extremely good for His Honour Judge Boyle —before whom the case is to be tried. Judge Boyle is a conceited and peppery judge whom Mr Truffle dislikes and an apoplectic fit is by no means out of the question.

But don't try to emulate Mr Trent. Your conference will be rather different. It will begin with Mr Truffle saying:

'I don't expect the defendant will turn up, but, if he does, you shouldn't have any difficulty.'

'He hasn't much of a defence anyway,' you say.

'He hasn't *any* defence,' gently corrects Mr Truffle. 'He's been debarred from defending.'

'Oh—yes—I see,' you begin. Probably you haven't

looked up to see how and why a person can be debarred from defending and what is the result.

Shortly afterwards Mr Truffle says that he must be going now and that he hopes you have everything you want.

'Oh yes, thank you,' you say.

'Well—that's fine,' says Mr Truffle. 'Your clerk tells me you'll be kind enough to give me a lift in your car. Perhaps you wouldn't mind picking me up at my office. It's on the way to the Court. Thank you so much. Goodbye.'

And before you can explain that your clerk has made a horrible mistake, and that you haven't got a car, Mr Truffle has gone. Clerks don't often make mistakes like that. But this time for once your clerk has done so. He has been so used to managing clerks briefing barristers by their cars rather than by their names that he might have noticed the difference on this occasion. Normally Mr Truffle, in ringing up to know if someone could do a case, would say :

'Is the Austin free on Monday for Shoreditch?' or 'I've got something for the Bentley on Tuesday at Ipswich,' or 'I've got a very small thing at Marylebone. The Standard will do.'

On this occasion he had said : 'Look, old man. I've got a tiny thing down at Lambeth. It'll hardly stand a fee. Have you got any new boys?'

'O.K. Ernie. I've got just the man for you. Keen as mustard.'

'Well—thanks old man. Tell him to pick me up at the office.'

'O.K.' says your clerk, absentmindedly—and forgets all about the matter.

Later, Mr Truffle is calling at the chambers and delivers the brief himself.

'Like to see him?' says the clerk. 'He's young, you know, but keen——' and your clerk makes a gesture to show how keen you are. It is to be hoped that it is justified.

15 *Conferences*

CONFERENCES are normally of three kinds. There is a conference when the legal executive of the solicitors who are briefing you, Mr Hope, just drops in for a quick piece of advice.

'Sorry to trouble you, Mr Green, but we're having difficulty in getting hold of one of the witnesses—Mr Skewbald. Wondered if you could do without him.'

It is a case where the plaintiff is claiming damages for fraud from your client, who is a motor car dealer. Mr Skewbald is the gentleman who actually sold the car to the plaintiff. The car broke down within half-an-hour of its being sold. Mr Skewbald, who is no longer in your client's employ, is alleged to have said all sorts of nice things about the car, in consequence of which the plaintiff is saying all sorts of less nice things about Mr Skewbald. If you are going to fight the case at all, Mr Skewbald is an essential witness.

'I'm afraid we shall have to have him,' you say. Even you know that.

'I told my principal you'd say that,' says Mr Hope. 'We've got to have him,' I said. 'Well, go and see Mr Green about it,' he said. 'Not much use having him if he doesn't want to come.' 'He'll have to tell the truth in the witness box,' I said. 'If he knows what it is,' my principal said. 'Which might mean anything, mightn't it?'

'Well,' you say, 'the plaintiff is going to say that Mr Skewbald said the car was in perfect condition and was a 1949 model, whereas it was in fact a 1940 model and, as far as I can see, in very imperfect condition. If we don't call Mr Skewbald to say that he said nothing of the kind, we're sunk.'

'Exactly what I said, Mr Green, exactly what I said.' He pauses a moment. 'D'you think we ought to settle the action, Mr Green?'

You can now see your only chance of a brief disappearing. All the same unfalteringly you say :

'If you can't get Mr Skewbald, you'll have to settle.'

It's painful, but it has to be done. If a case is settled after the brief has been delivered counsel is entitled to his fee, whether the case is settled or not. Your brief has not been delivered, but tradition is too strong for you. It is traditional at the Bar (and the tradition is only broken by a few practitioners of doubtful repute) that counsel does everything he can to save his client money, even at the expense of his own pocket. No reputable counsel tries to keep a case going in order to earn fees. Often, what could turn out to be a very heavy case, entitling counsel to large fees, is settled at a very early stage on the advice of counsel. Lawyers are not popular among the public as a whole, but there is no doubt whatever that all reputable barristers and solicitors do everything they can to save their clients from litigation and expense.

'Very well,' says Mr Hope, 'I'll tell my principal what you say—but it's only what I told him.'

That is what might be called the unofficial conference or 'a word.' Your clerk will not charge a fee for it. Not at this stage anyway.

Then there is the pre-arranged conference without the client. This is attended by the solicitor or his legal executive. Don't forget that in litigation the legal

executive is a very important person to you. In your
early days many of them will terrify you into doing
all sorts of things which should be against your better
judgment. Try not to give in. But the only things which
can give you confidence are experience and knowledge.
Only time can give you the former but you can do a
good deal yourself to acquire the latter. Don't be led
into agreeing with a proposition unless you know it's
right. Either look it up then and there or say that you'll
do so later. Suppose, for example, you're having a conference about a case in the County Court. Your
solicitor client says :

'Well, they're not relying on breach of warranty in
their defence. So they won't be able to, unless the judge
gives them leave to amend. And I can't see him doing
that at that late stage, can you, Mr Green?'

Well, to begin with, you've no idea whether the judge
will or will not give leave to amend in any particular
case at any particular time. Such knowledge can only
come from experience. But have you looked up the
provisions in the County Court rules about defences
and amendments and so forth? The chances are that
you have not. If you had, you would have discovered
that a defendant is entitled to rely on any defence at
the trial, whether he has put it in his written defence
or not. All the judge can do is to adjourn the case and
order the defendant to pay the costs. He cannot refuse
to let him rely on the new defence. Supposing, then,
you had agreed with your solicitor and said—as many
practitioners would have done——

'Well, of course, it is a question of discretion. I can't
guarantee that the judge won't give him leave.'

Later on in Court the defendant seeks to rely on
breach of warranty. You leap to your feet :

Wigs and Gowns
or
Brothers in Law

'But, your Honour, he hasn't pleaded breach of warranty.'

'Well, he's relying on it now,' says Judge Twist.

'But as a matter of discretion, your Honour,' you say, 'I ask you to say that he shall not be allowed to do so.'

'It's not a matter of discretion at all, Mr Green,' says the judge.

Probably you say :

'I submit it is, your Honour.'

If you do—the judge sighs and says :

'Have you ever looked at Order 9 Rule 8, Mr Green? If not, I suggest you do so.'

Not a very pretty picture on your first appearance in court for this particular solicitor. How much better to have looked up the rules at the conference and found out about it. But very few young barristers do. A good many practitioners in the County Court are wholly unaware of the existence of Order 9 Rule 8. Look it up.

It is quite true that to look up something during a conference may delay matters, and in your early days you may feel awkward doing it under the eye of your solicitor. But that can't be helped. Think how much more awkward it may be in Court later on if you don't. Experienced practitioners never mind looking up points in the presence of their clients.

Then there is the conference with the lay client. In a case where there is a serious issue of fact this conference is of great importance, and you should cross-examine your client thoroughly—putting all the questions you think might be put by counsel on the other side when cross-examining. But do it pleasantly, or your client may ask :

'Are you on my side, or on theirs?'

If, as a result of your cross-examination, you discover

that your case is really hopeless, you should advise your clients accordingly and tell them to settle it as best they can. If your client actually admits that his former version was untrue and that his claim or defence, as the case may be, is without foundation then, of course, you cannot go on with the case. This subject is dealt with at greater length in Chapter 20.

16 *Judge or Master in Chambers*

A GREAT deal of a junior's work takes place before the Judge or Master in Chambers. As you know, the appearances before Judge and Master in chambers relate mainly to the intermediate stages of an action—applications for injunctions, requests for particulars of a defence or statement of claim, discovery of documents and so on. It is on these occasions that the practitioner with the wide knowledge of the practice is supreme. It is surprising how comparatively few practitioners in the High Court or County Court really master the practice. Of course it takes years to get to that stage, but most practitioners go through as many years without mastering it. That is because they have not set about it methodically from the beginning. That is the only way in which it can be done. It will be of inestimable advantage to you, if you make up your mind to do it. It is not in the least difficult but it does require patience and persistence and a good deal of work.

Certain practitioners become well known for nearly always winning their applications before Master or Judge. This is not just because the Master and Judge are influenced by the fact that they know that the counsel in question probably know more about the practice than they do. It is because, owing to their great knowledge, they seldom make an application which is

Before a Master in Chambers
or
Where some of the money goes

not justified or resist an application which ought to be granted. There are some barristers who through stupidity and obstinacy almost make a point of honour of refusing any request by the other side in the course of a case. This very seldom does their clients any good and often does them harm. The sensible and able practitioner normally makes a point of giving his opponent everything he asks for, unless the request is wholly unjustified. If there is a doubt about it, in the ordinary way give the other side the benefit of it. Within reason, give him all the particulars he asks for and show him all the documents he wants to see. Holding things back, even if you are technically entitled to do so, will not in the ordinary way help your case.

In your early days you will find that, when you are against able and experienced practitioners before the Judge or Master in Chambers, you usually lose. It is entirely up to you to see that this state of affairs comes to an end. If you find that you are constantly losing applications in Chambers after a few years' practice, you can be pretty certain that it is your fault. When you know your job, you will not advise applications which are not likely to succeed and you will not advise resisting applications which ought to succeed. Until your clients get to know you well, you may have some tussles with them on the subject. Some solicitors, like some barristers, are apt to dispute with the other side as often as they can. They suspect every request and refuse to grant it. It is your job to step on that sort of thing.

'Why shouldn't we give the particulars, Mr Spoon?'

'But, sir, they refused when we asked.'

'I dare say they did, but they had to give them in the end.'

'But I told them on the telephone that they could issue a summons.'

'Well, telephone them again and say I've advised you to give them.'

This advice may have saved your client up to £50 or so.

If you find that your master loses about as many summonses as he wins, you can be quite sure that, as far as practice and procedure go, he is of a pretty low standard. So profit by his mistakes. There are some summonses which are merely procedural and cannot be won or lost, but of those which can be won or lost the able and experienced practitioner should win at least four for every one lost. That, indeed, is a conservative estimate.

A similar criterion exists in regard to serious allegations, such as fraud. Such allegations should not be made unless they are likely to succeed and if they are really likely to succeed they will succeed far more often than they fail. Obviously there will be occasions when you are justified in making a serious allegation and it fails, but if you have taken proper precautions before making such allegations (i.e., if necessary sent for your client and cross-examined him, drafted letters for your solicitor to send to the parties concerned, told your solicitors to take detailed proofs from witnesses and so forth), if you have done all these things and it still seems right that the allegation should be made, then usually it will succeed. So, if you find that your master is failing in actions where he is alleging fraud on behalf of his client as often as he is succeeding, you may be pretty sure that he is making mistakes. And, if you find that you have the same experience, remember that the fault is in all probability yours. If statistics were available for juniors of the highest credentials, you would find that they seldom put forward serious allegations on behalf of their clients which did not succeed. Make up your mind to do the same yourself. That doesn't mean to say that you are to be frightened of making allegations, however serious. You must be prepared on behalf of your client to do or say anything that can properly be said or done. But it does mean that you are to exercise very great care before you do or say it.

17 *Opinions*

WHEN you are asked for your opinion give it. That sounds obvious but, if you had read the opinions of some counsel, you would understand what is meant. For example :

'In this case I am asked to advise whether——'

There then follow ten lines taken straight out of the solicitor's instructions. Mr Trent complained of his solicitor merely repeating proofs in his instructions. Solicitors might reasonably complain of barristers merely repeating the instructions which they have been given. Everyone knows that you have been asked to advise whether in the circumstances Mr Jones has a claim against his neighbour for nuisance. What most solicitors want in your written opinion is your opinion—not a recitation of the facts, which they already know and which they have already taken the trouble to set out in writing. Some solicitors, however, do like this method and that, no doubt, is the reason why some counsel of repute adopt it.

Where the facts are not set out in full in the instructions but have to be culled from various documents sent down with those instructions, different considerations, of course, apply. It may be very useful then to set out a resumé of the facts on which your opinion is based. Moreover, if you choose for ease of reading to set out succinctly the substance of each question in one or two words before your answer, that is quite different and may be helpful. For example :

'I answer the questions put to me as follows :

1. Is A liable to B? Yes—my reasons are as follows :
2. Damages : In my view the damages likely to be recovered will be between £x and £y.' (Then follow your reasons.)

Moreover, where you are giving an opinion for the purpose of the Legal Aid Committee deciding whether to grant your client legal aid, it is desirable to set out the facts on which your opinion is based, as this saves the Committee from having to read the instructions which you have received, as well as your opinion. The same remarks apply to a case where an infant is involved and the approval of the Court is required for a suggested compromise and your opinion is going to be shown to the Court.

But the above suggestions only relate to verbosity, and are far less important than the next point. The opinion goes on as follows :

'The question I am asked is a difficult one. On the one hand there are the decisions X, Y and Z, which suggest etc. Then there are the decisions A, B and C, which suggest something rather different, namely etc. On the whole I think it probable that the judge at the trial might be inclined to follow the former line of decisions rather than the latter, but, of course, he might not. And then a great deal will depend on the way in which the case is presented and what the witness Blank will say.'

In other words, the opinion waffles on, undoubtedly calling attention to salient points in the case but leaving out the one thing counsel is being asked for—his opinion. Your opinion may not be very valuable in your first years, but, if you are being paid for it, give it. In other words make up your mind. If it is a question of law, how would you decide it if you were the judge? That is your opinion. It may, of course, be that your opinion will be contrary to a certain decided case. Then, of course, it is right to say that the judge may choose to follow that case rather than your submission and that, unless your client is prepared to go to the Court of Appeal, there may be no point in his fighting the case.

When your opinion is required on a question of fact, it will naturally depend on whether the witnesses are believed. But you should be able to form an opinion on the material before you of what is likely to happen. In your earlier days you may have difficulty in forming a very valuable opinion. The ability to do this can only come from experience. But try from the start. Force your mind to come to conclusions, but don't do this by making a jab at it.

One of the most important part of your duties as a junior will be to advise as to the evidence to be called in a case. In practically every case in the High Court and in many cases in the County Court, an advice on evidence will be required. If there is a good advice on evidence and a good solicitor, your client's case will have the best opportunity of success. In the process of advising on evidence you have to consider most carefully everything that must be done to have your case in apple-pie order when the day of trial arrives. You will advise that all the necessary witnesses should be interviewed and, if necessary, subpoenaed, that all the necessary documents should be secured, all the necessary enquiries made and so on. If there are difficult questions likely to be asked of some of your witnesses in cross-examination, draw attention to them in your advice, so that you will know what the answer is going to be and the witness will be prepared for the question. It is not normally proper for you to interview the witnesses other than your own client and expert witnesses, but it is not only proper but most important that in your advice you should draw attention to points which your solicitor should ask them. To give a good advice on evidence you should fight the case in advance.

Sometimes you will be discouraged by the fact that, although you have taken immense trouble to provide your solicitor with a near-perfect advice on evidence, the brief is eventually delivered to you in a form which shows that very little notice has been taken of what you have written. Well, of course, it is discouraging, but you must not let it interfere with the way you do your work—even with the same solicitors. Except perhaps to this extent. The next time you give an advice to the same solicitors, remind them of what happened on the last occasion and try to persuade them to improve on that performance.

All good solicitors take most careful note of your advice on evidence, and in many cases, if you see it later, you will find ticks placed against the various paragraphs, to indicate that the procedure advised has been adopted.

In your advice on evidence you should also advise on the arrangement and presentation of the documents for the Court, e.g. whether there should be one or two or more bundles of correspondence, whether the other documents should be bundled together or separately and so on. All bundles of correspondence and documents should be paged and a top copy must be available for use of the judge. As often as not today, a carbon or photostat copy is handed to the judge and, while many judges will not mind if it is really legible, there may be

Witness box at a London Magistrate's Court
or
'I swear by the Almighty God'

an explosion if the judge is given a blurred fifth carbon or an illegible photo-copy while counsel cheerfully reads from the top copy. Again, it must be emphasized that the judge is not going to decide against you because you give him an unnumbered, smudged carbon copy of correspondence, but he may very well say things to you which in your early stages may seriously unsettle you, and, if you are feeling that you want to go home to mother, you may not feel capable of presenting your client's case in the best possible light. When you are more experienced, you will ensure that such things don't happen. And it is in the advice on evidence that you can tell your solicitor exactly how to prepare the case for presentation in Court. It is you who have to present it, not he. And he does not therefore always realise the importance of everything being in perfect order. Of course first-class solicitors of experience know these things. But there are plenty of young and inexperienced solicitors.

One thing you must never forget. The person whom you are representing is the lay client. He must always come first. You must never save your solicitor at the expense of the lay client. In your early days you may be very much tempted to do so, and it will be very surprising if you do not succumb to the temptation. But you ought not to do so, and you are letting down your profession if you do.

18 *The Leading Question*

ONE of the most difficult things you will be called on to do is to examine your own witness. Examination-in-chief, as it is called, is popularly supposed to be much simpler than cross-examination. Advocates are referred to with awe as 'great cross-examiners.' Well, of course, there is a very considerable art in cross-examination but, as a general rule, examination-in-chief is much harder than cross-examination—particularly if your witness tends to be hostile or stupid or forgetful. In examination-in-chief you must not ask leading questions.

Few members of the public know what a leading question is and a substantial number of legal practitioners have an incorrect notion of its meaning. You often hear people parry difficult questions in ordinary conversation by calling them—quite wrongly—leading questions.

'Are you going to marry the girl?'

'Ah, that's a leading question.'

Well, it isn't.

Leading questions are not permissible in examining your own witness because in effect they put the answer into the witness's mouth. Here is an example of the evidence of the petitioner in an undefended divorce. Time after time the Court of Appeal has complained at the way leading questions are asked in these cases, but, if one may judge from the number of times the complaint is repeated, with little result. The reason is that, as the case is not defended, there is no one on the other side to object to the question and some commissioners do not intervene, although they ought to do so. Evidence obtained in the following way is almost valueless.

Question : Is your name Dorabella Beta?

Answer : Yes.

Question : Where do you live, Mrs Beta?

Answer : At 1, Omicron Buildings, Sigma Square, N.W.2.

Question : Were you married on the 14th day of October 1947 to Samuel Beta at the Gamma Register Office in the County of Lambda, when your maiden name was Omega?

Answer : Yes.

Question : I think there are no children of the marriage?

Answer : No.

Question : Was your marriage a happy one?

Answer : No.

Question : Was that because your husband beat you?

Answer : Yes.

Question : Did he use foul language towards you?

Answer : Yes.

Question : Did he keep you short of money?

Answer : Yes.

Question : Did he come in late two or three nights in the week?

Answer : Yes.

Question : And if you asked him where he had been did he hit you?

Answer : Yes.

Question : Hard?

Answer : Yes.

Question : Where did he hit you?

Answer : Round the head.

Question : And all over the body?

Answer : Yes.

Question : Did your health suffer in consequence?

Answer : Yes.

Question : Eventually you left him?

Answer : Yes.

Question : Has your health been better since then?

Answer : Yes.

Counsel : If your Lordship is satisfied, I ask for a decree nisi with costs.

Commissioner : Decree nisi with costs.

There were only three non-leading questions in that examination, and one was as to the petitioner's address. (Incidentally, the number of wives in undefended divorces whose husbands hit them 'round the head' is quite extraordinary. Not in the face or on the head, but 'round the head'.)

Evidence obtained in that way is obviously unsatisfactory. It should be obtained without counsel in effect putting the words into his witness's mouth.

A leading question is normally defined as a question which itself suggests the answer. That is correct as far as it goes, but it is insufficient. The question : 'Was anything said about Premium Bonds?' does not necessarily suggest the answer 'Yes' or 'No'. Yet the question could be a grossly leading question.

It is often not appreciated by lawyers that whether or not a question is leading depends on the circumstances in which it is asked. Here is a simple example. In an action between A and B a vital issue is whether sausages were mentioned at a particular conversation. It is A's case that they were mentioned, B's that they were not. A witness is called on behalf of A. He gives evidence of the conversation, but says nothing about sausages. A's counsel has a proof from the witness in which he says quite definitely that sausages were mentioned but in the witness-box he gives details of everything that he remembers being said but leaves out the essential sausages. The dialogue will proceed something like this :

A's COUNSEL (sweating): Now, Mr Jones, was anything else said?

B's COUNSEL : I hope my learned friend isn't going to lead.

A's COUNSEL (*who up to the moment has not led but does not know how he's going to adduce the vital evidence without doing so*): Really! this is too bad. That was a perfectly proper question.

B's COUNSEL : I only wanted to be sure about the next one.

A's COUNSEL : Will my learned friend kindly refrain from interrupting unless I give him cause. Now, Mr Jones, was anything else said at this conversation?

WITNESS : Anything else?

A's COUNSEL : Yes.

WITNESS : About what?

A's COUNSEL : About anything.

WITNESS : D'you mean more than I've said already?

A's COUNSEL : Yes—sir, something besides what you've said already.

WITNESS : At that conversation?

A's COUNSEL : Yes—at that conversation.

WITNESS : Something else?

A's COUNSEL : Yes—something else.

WITNESS : Such as?

A's COUNSEL : That's for you to tell the learned judge, Mr Jones. I mustn't suggest it to you.

WITNESS : That makes it very difficult.

A's COUNSEL : Take your time—just think.

B's COUNSEL (menacingly) : Now——

A's COUNSEL : I'm perfectly entitled to invite the witness to think.

WITNESS : Perhaps if you could just tell me what you want me to say.

Well, that is exactly what A's counsel may not do and were he to ask : 'Was anything said about sausages?' it would be a grossly leading and most improper question. Yet it will be shown in a moment that precisely the same question asked in different circumstances would not be leading at all. Meantime you may ask what will happen if A's counsel does ask the improper question. Well, after the storm has died down and counsel has been reproved by the judge, the witness may say :

WITNESS : Oh—yes, of course we mentioned the sausages.

JUDGE : Why didn't you say so before? You were asked if anything else was said.

WITNESS : I forgot, my Lord. I've not given evidence before and it's surprising how everything goes out of one's head.

Well, now it's up to the judge to decide whether the witness genuinely forgot something that did happen, or whether he just forgot to *say* something which did not happen—for the evidence has been given, even though it was given as the result of an improper question.

This happens more often than it should.

It is one of the most difficult tasks of the advocate to steer an awkward witness through the witness-box without impropriety and with success. Only advocates in the highest class can do it. In the example just quoted such an advocate, instead of asking a leading question, would probably have taken the witness to some other matter which might recall the sausages to his mind. For example :

COUNSEL : Well, we'll leave that interview for the moment. D'you remember a later interview with Mr Smith—in the late summer?

WITNESS : When I told him about the sausages, d'you mean?

COUNSEL : What sausages?

WITNESS : The ones I was just telling you about.

COUNSEL : But you haven't told us anything about sausages.

WITNESS : Well, of course, at that interview you were asking me about I mentioned the sausages.

The advantage of obtaining the evidence in this way is not simply that it is properly instead of improperly obtained, but also that the effect of the witness's evidence on the judge's mind is likely to be much greater if the first mention of sausages comes from him rather than from counsel.

When you have discovered an advocate who is able to conduct an examination-in-chief like this—your master or someone else—watch him and see how he does it. You will find that he extracts the maximum amount of evidence out of his witness without once asking an improperly leading question. Of course, there are times when leading questions are not improper, e.g. on formal matters or matters which are not in dispute. Indeed, counsel will often say to his opponent : 'You may lead about that.' The object of this is, of course, to save time. But, apart from formal matters and matters not in dispute, you must never lead your own witness and you must not forget that the mere fact that

The Divorce Court
or
'He was always hitting me round the head'

the witness could answer 'Yes' or 'No' to the question does not prevent it from being leading.

It is difficult to define exactly what a leading question is, so as to include all classes of leading questions, but probably 'a question which itself suggests the answer or unfairly leads the mind of the witness to a particular subject' is somewhere near the mark. The important word is *unfairly*. You are entitled to bring anything to the witness's mind provided it is done fairly. But in the case quoted, the issue being whether sausages were mentioned, to ask that witness whether they were mentioned was plainly unfair and therefore 'leading.' Some able advocates, who are normally perfectly fair in the conduct of their practice, will in the heat of battle ask leading questions when they should not. Their enthusiasm or anxiety has got the better of them. But the top-class advocates do not. There are not so very many of them.

The witness having said eventually that sausages were mentioned, suppose that B's counsel in due course calls a witness to show that sausages were not mentioned. First of all he asks the witness what was said during the conversation. The witness gives his account and (if he gives evidence in accordance with his proof) says nothing about sausages. When he has finished his account, B's counsel can quite properly ask him the very same question which it was improper for A's counsel to ask.

'Was anything said about sausages?' The question asked in these circumstances neither suggests the answer nor brings the subject *unfairly* to the witness' mind. That is because the witness is called in support of the party who is alleging that *nothing* was said about sausages. You will only learn the difference between leading and non-leading questions by experience, but you should bear in mind the examples just given and remember that the mere fact that a question ends with an 'or not' does not prevent it from being a leading question. 'Were sausages mentioned or not?' would in A's counsel's mouth be just as objectionable as 'Were sausages mentioned?'

In cross-examination, of course, leading questions are permitted as much as you like. It is possibly due to the fact that such leading questions are sometimes awkward questions that the general public makes the mistake referred to at the beginning of this chapter. Whether he was going to marry the girl may well have been an awkward question, but it was not a leading one.

The difficulty of examining a witness is to some extent reduced, if you can rely implicitly on the proof taken by the solicitor from that witness. Normally the only witnesses you see are your lay client and perhaps an expert witness. You therefore have no chance of questioning your other witnesses on their statements. Very much depends, therefore, on the care which has been taken by the solicitor or his managing clerk in obtaining their proofs.

If you succeed at the Bar you will in course of time come across every variety of proof-taker, from the pretty disreputable solicitor's clerk, who tells the witness what to say (true or false), to the first-class solicitor who takes a proof with great care to ascertain exactly what the witness intends to say on all material matters, whether they are in favour of your client or not. The Law Society does all it can to keep the reputation of solicitors high, and it is indeed very high, but it has so far been found impossible to avoid the existence in the profession of some unqualified clerks who are not as scrupulous as they should be. And a few worse then that. And they may be employed by a perfectly reputable solicitor who has not noticed anything wrong with them.

They are mentioned now so that you may be on your guard. It is very difficult for the young barrister to hold his own with a solicitor or legal executive in his early days. He is usually so terrified of offending them. But, although courtesy should be your watchword both in and out of Court, you must draw a hard and fast line between proper and improper conduct and, once you are satisfied that your client is on the wrong side of the line, you must either get rid of him or tell him so in no uncertain terms. That will probably have the same effect. But you must do it.

19 *Hardy Annual*

IT is easy enough for a guilty man to be acquitted but very difficult for an innocent man to succeed in being convicted. But no doubt one or two who have tried hard enough have brought it off. That is not entirely a cynical way of putting it. Probably most of the innocent people who have been found guilty have been convicted because of the lies they have told, and those lies have usually been told because, although innocent of the charge on which they were eventually tried, they were committing some other crime at the time. Thinking that proof of such an alibi would not be altogether to their advantage they invent a false one. The jury can hardly be blamed for convicting them if the alibi put forward was transparently false and the prisoner lied in the witness-box in support of it.

Juries have not the same experience as judges in sorting out the lies which emerge from the witness-box. Plenty of people with good cases try to improve on them by telling lies or half-truths. If they lose a case as a result, they have no right to complain, but a judge does try to decide a case correctly in spite of any lies which either party may have told him. Judges know that some witnesses only have to be asked a question by cross-examining counsel to say 'No' to it, if they think counsel wants them to say 'Yes,' quite irrespective of the truth.

Here is a question which you will undoubtedly ask at some stage in your career:

'Now, Mr Jones, have you not discussed this case with your son and daughter?'

'Certainly not.'

'I suggest that you have.'

'I have not.'

'But you live in the same house as they do.'

'So what?'

'You see them at meals?'

'Of course I do.'

'Well, the case was of interest to you and them, wasn't it?'

'Not really.'

'I suggest it was of great interest.'

'I'm on my oath.'

'I know you are, Mr Jones, and I suggest that it is quite untrue that you didn't talk to your son and daughter about the case.'

'Never said I didn't talk to them about it.'

'You certainly did.'

'I didn't.'

'You said you'd never discussed the case with your son and daughter.'

'Nor we have.'

'But you've just admitted that you have.'

'I've done no such thing.'

'Really, Mr Jones, his Lordship isn't deaf, you know, nor am I. You said you'd talked to your son and daughter about the case.'

'Well, of course we have. Nothing wrong in that is there?'

'Certainly not—it's what I should expect. But you swore you hadn't discussed it.'

'Well, we didn't.'

Cross-examing the witness
or
'Do yourself justice, Mr Jones'

'Oh—you distinguish between "talk about" and "discuss," do you?'

'I don't distinguish anything. I don't know what it's got to do with the case.'

Well, that is just an example of a well-known theme. Mr Jones was pretty honest in that case. But he considered, as do many witnesses, that this type of cross-examination is designed to show that he and his witnesses have put their heads together to tell a lot of lies. Many of the stupider witnesses will persist in saying that they have never talked about the case or even mentioned it to someone with whom they must in fact have had many conversations on the subject. But they think the admission will hurt them in the case and they lie like troopers to avoid making it.

In your earlier days when you have successfully embarked on this line of cross-examination and triumphantly persuaded the witness to lie on the subject you will feel a little aggrieved when the judge replies to your passionate address with :

'Well, you know, many of them do that, Mr Green.'

Hotly you reply : 'But, your Honour, he's told a lie on oath. He's committed perjury. It was quite deliberate. I asked him several times !'

'I know,' says the judge, with a sigh. 'It's a pity'— and decides against you.

That does not mean to say that you may not win a case if a vital witness tells a deliberate lie, but it does mean that there is no automatic rule on the subject.

20 *What Do You Do When You Know Your Client is Guilty?*

EVERY lawyer is asked this question and, though the answer is comparatively simple, it is not always so simple to know where your duty lies in any particular case.

The normal answer to this question is, of course, that in civil or criminal cases you must not put forward what you *know* to be a false case. But *know* means *know* and not *think*. You can only *know* your client is putting forward a false case if he tells you so himself. If you only think he is guilty, that is no reason for not defending him. It is what the magistrate or jury thinks which matters. You are not trying him. They are. If barristers had to refuse to defend a man because they thought he was guilty very few of those accused of crime would be defended at all.[1]

[1] Dr Johnson is reported as saying something similar, in much better language, nearly 200 years ago:

BOSWELL: But what do you think of supporting a cause which you know to be bad?

JOHNSON: Sir, you do not know it to be good or bad till the judge determines it. I have said that you are to state facts fairly; so that your thinking, or what you call knowing, a cause to be bad, must be from reasoning, must be from your supposing your arguments to be weak and inconclusive. But, Sir, that is not enough. An argument which does not convince yourself, may convince the Judge to whom you urge it; and if it does convince him, why, then, Sir, you are wrong and he is right. It is his business to judge; and you are not to be confident in your own opinion that a cause is bad, but to say all you can for your client, and then hear the judge's opinion.

Boswell's *Life of Johnson*, Everyman Edition.
Vol. 1 p. 342.

If in a criminal case your client persists in proclaiming his innocence, however strong the evidence is against him, you not only have a right but a duty to go on defending him. In a civil case you would be entitled to refuse to act for a client if you were satisfied by over-whelming evidence that your client was telling you lies. But even in such a case you would be entitled to appear for him provided you did not in any way seek to cover up the nakedness of your case. The rules as to your duties are different in civil and criminal cases. It is so im-portant that a man should not be wrongly deprived of his liberty that, short of actually being told by your client that he is guilty, you are entitled to do your best in support of his plea of Not Guilty if he himself persists in it and denies his guilt to you. In civil cases although you are, of course, entitled to put forward a bad case on behalf of your client if he insists that it is the truth, the stage is more easily reached when an advocate who is personally satisfied as to the in-justice of his case is entitled to withdraw from it. 'Who is personally satisfied' does not mean 'who knows.' It is something less than that.

All that is well settled. It is also settled that, even if your client in a criminal case tells you he is guilty, you can allow him to plead Not Guilty and see if the case is proved against him. You must not in such a case suggest that he is not guilty, but you may submit that his guilt is not proved.

What is not so simple is to apply the rule to every case without compromising your conscience. Suppose your client in a criminal case says to you :

'Do you want me to tell the truth?'

You, no doubt, say : 'Yes, of course.' But suppose in such a case you felt satisfied, having regard to the

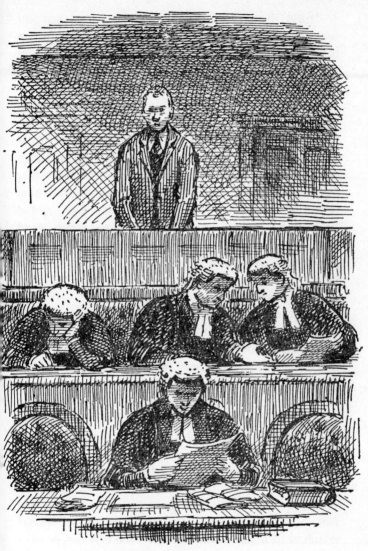

Prisoner in the Dock
or
'I'd better say guilty'

evidence, that he is in fact guilty and that his pro-
testations of innocence are false, how hard do you try
to persuade him to tell you the truth? How fiercely
do you cross-examine him in conference? The answer
is—certainly in most cases—that you should treat him
just like any other client. If in fact he breaks down
under your private cross-examination and confesses his
guilt it is in all probability to his advantage. Instead of
putting up a false defence he will plead Guilty and may
receive a lesser sentence in consequence. On the other
hand, if he does not break down, the cross-examination
will have helped to prepare him for the trial, and if
he happens to be innocent, that will be a very good
thing. If he is in fact guilty, he will be one of the many
guilty men who profit from the English idea that it is
better for a hundred guilty men to be acquitted than
for one innocent man to be convicted.

It is thought by some people that a barrister avoids
asking his client directly whether he is guilty, lest he
may confess and deprive himself of the right to be
defended (except to the very limited extent already mentioned or on the question of sentence). This is a wrong
impression. It is true that there has been at least one
well-known barrister who refused to see his client in
serious criminal cases (possibly for this reason) but this
is most unusual.

There may be an exceptional case where you might
be justified in acting differently, but normally you
should ask your client all the awkward questions you
can think of. It is not your duty to try to procure the
acquittal of a guilty man but to do the best you possibly
can to secure the acquittal of a man who tells you
he is innocent. If in the process he confesses, no in-
justice is done. In the days when there was a death

penalty for murder some counsel treated their client charged with this offence rather more gently. This no doubt was on the principle that human life is so sacred that it was better to risk some slight damage to their sense of morality or their consciences than the irrevocable damage to their clients if they persuaded them to be hanged.

21 *Junior and Q.C.*

In *Brothers in Law* the film company made an elementary mistake in referring to Mr Grimes, who was a busy junior barrister, as a Q.C. This was not done in the film itself but on the credit titles and in the leaflets which the company distributed to the Press. So nearly all the reviews of that film refer to Mr Grimes as a Q.C. All lawyers realised the mistake, as a Q.C. cannot take pupils.

The mistake arose because the film company's directors thought, no doubt as many others do, that every important barrister is a Q.C. They did not know that barristers are divided into juniors and Q.C.s. And, if you have not taken silk, you are a junior. But to remain a junior does not mean that you are of small importance. Many junior barristers become Circuit judges and a few become High Court judges without ever becoming a Q.C. In 1958 there were two Lords Justices of Appeal who never became 'silks.'

Everyone starts as a junior and the majority remain juniors for the rest of their time. It by no means follows that those who become Q.C.s do better than those who remain juniors. On the contrary, many juniors have a far larger income than some Q.C.s. The difference between a junior and a Q.C. is really this—that a junior does all the work which a barrister can do, i.e. all the paper work and the court work too. Whereas a Q.C. for the most part only does court work. He certainly

gives opinions from time to time and he may be taken
into consultation over drafting some important pleading, but this is only a tiny proportion of the paper work
which a junior does.

The result is that a most successful junior may fail
as a Q.C. There have been instances of juniors earning
£10,000 per annum before the 1939 war taking silk
and earning £2,000 or less. The reason is that a barrister may be very good at paper work and adequate in
court. Once he becomes a Q.C. he gives up his paper
work and adequacy in court may not be enough for a
Q.C. Hence the taking of silk is nearly always a problem and it may be a very serious risk. Moreover, as a
Q.C. cannot normally appear in Court without a junior
as well, many cases will not stand the extra expense of
employing two counsel instead of one. In consequence
there may be a dearth of work for all but the most
successful Q.C.s.

Don't think, because there is a Q.C. on one side and
only a junior on the other, that the junior's client is
necessarily at a disadvantage. It may be just the opposite. And, indeed, a junior's fee may be higher than a
Q.C.'s. A Q.C., who had not much work, might be
pleased to go into court for £52.50, whereas a very
busy junior might refuse to take the case for less than
£105. But, if you succeed as a Q.C., your gross income
will be much higher than a junior's, and you may
get a little extra leisure in view of the absence of paper
work. It is also more usual for High Court Judges to
be appointed from silks than from juniors.

In order to become a Q.C. you have to apply to the
Lord Chancellor asking him to recommend you to Her
Majesty for appointment as one of Her Counsel. There
is a custom that, if you are a Member of Parliament,

F

and have been called a sufficiently long time, your application will be granted automatically, but, apart from that special case, applications are normally only granted to those who are sufficiently well known in the courts in which they practise to justify the appointment, or who are higher Civil Servants in Government legal departments or, occasionally, university professors. They must, of course, be of unquestioned integrity. If the Lord Chancellor refuses a request one year he may grant it another. This might happen if, when you first applied, there were already enough silks practising in your class of work. But by the time you are even considering the question of taking silk you won't need any advice from this book.

Silk and Junior
or
'*I should have thought this was worth putting to her*'

22 *The Two Mr Greens*

ONE day, when you are a pupil, you may go down to the Old Bailey or to London Sessions, either because your master happens to have a criminal case or because you want to go and have a look. It ought only to be for the former reason. You have little enough time in a year as a pupil to learn your job and it is usually a waste of time to go into Court, unless you go with someone who has a brief there and unless you have yourself read that brief carefully. After your pupillage, if there is nothing better to do, it may be of some use to go into Court to study the habits of the various judges and their various foibles. But during your pupillage there ought always to be something better to do if your master has a reasonable practice. There are, however, young men who think it will be amusing to trot down to the Old Bailey instead of sitting, for the third day perhaps, in a not very interesting case about cocoa beans and bills of lading, which is rather above their heads. These young men are unlikely to succeed at the Bar. You will certainly find that a good deal of the work is above your head if your master is in substantial practice, and it is up to you to develop your faculties and knowledge so that you can understand as much about everything as possible.

When you first come to the Bar you will see large briefs—possibly even a foot high—delivered to your master, and you may wonder how on earth you are ever going to understand a case of that size. You may well ask yourself how it is possible to cope with such a voluminous set of papers and do the other work there is to be done as well. It would appear to take hours or days merely to read all the documents, let alone to sort out the issues involved and consider the law. It is to be hoped you do feel like that, and if you do, and if you are prepared to do the necessary work that has already been mentioned, you need not feel at all discouraged.

Gradually you will find that you can master even the largest and most complicated cases. Of course it will take time—of course you couldn't possibly master a large or difficult case satisfactorily in your first year or two. But, if you persevere, you will find that you will be doing it automatically. And in time the size of a brief will have no terrors for you, though on occasions you may want to ensure that your clerk is charging enough. As matter of fact he is likely to charge enough if the papers are bulky. Clerks don't exactly charge so much a pound weight, but to some extent they do go by size. It is in fact when the papers are comparatively small in size that the clerk may be about to undercharge, until you tell him that far more work is involved in them than the mere size would suggest. You have previously been told to leave the question of fees to the clerk and you may wonder therefore at this reference to a barrister discussing a fee with his clerk. That will be at a much later stage when you are a junior with a large practice. At that stage you will, of course, do what you please and it would be impertinent to tell you how to conduct your practice.

In the old days it might have happened that you obtained a dock brief. Today, as I have already mentioned, Legal Aid has virtually ousted the dock brief, though it is theoretically still possible for a prisoner who has £2.25 to ask to be represented by any counsel in court who is not employed on a case. Let us assume that it happens to you. You go down to the cells to see your client. He greets you cheerfully.

'Well, well,' he says, 'that's a good sign. My name's Green too.'

'Good afternoon,' you say. 'Can you tell me what your case is all about?'

'Now that's a question,' sayd Mr Green. 'You're pretty new to this game, aren't you?'

'I'm afraid so.'

'Don't apologise, sir, don't apologise. We all have to start sometime. Let me see, how long ago was my first case——?' He thinks for a moment or two. 'Ah—that's going back a bit. Before you were born anyway.'

'And did you win it?' you ask politely.

'Now that's what some people call a leading question,' says Mr Green, 'but I know that it isn't. I've not been here ten times for nothing.'

'Ten times at the Old Bailey?' you ask with some horror.

'Don't upset yourself. Another ten at the Sessions too—not to mention a jaunt or two before the beaks. But you ought to be pleased. Don't have to ride me in blinkers. I know what's the other side of the rails— and who's in the grandstand too. And I'm not put off by the cheering either—if I get off.'

'Have they actually cheered you?' you ask in some astonishment.

'I'll tell you,' says Mr Green. 'It was stopped pretty quickly of course, but they just couldn't help it. Now it was like this——'

'Don't you think it would be better to tell me about your present case?' you say.

'Quite positively no,' says Mr Green, 'I don't. We'll have quite enough about that later. Let's enjoy ourselves for the moment.'

'But the case may come on,' you persist.

'Keep calm, sir, keep calm,' Mr Green says soothingly. 'You just say you're not ready. Then they can't begin. Wouldn't be fair, would it? Justice must not only be done—between you and me I'm not so sure that I always agree with that part—but must manifestly be seen to be done. You know who said that, I suppose?'

'Was it Lord Hewart?' you ask timidly.

'Good for you, boy—I beg your pardon, sir. You'll do well. You've got a memory. Lord Hewart it was. I did him a good turn once. Like to hear?'

'Well really,' you say, 'I must know something about your case.'

'There you go again. Like two-year-olds—go all jittery when you get near the starter. But then, of course, that's what you are. Now I'm what they call aged. D'you know what that means?'

'Elderly, I suppose,' you say.

'Well, that's right in a way. But what it means is seven or over—racing parlance.'

'I'm sorry,' you say, 'I don't know anything about racing.'

'Pity,' says Mr Green. 'I could have given you a good thing for a seller up at Catterick tomorrow. You wouldn't like to put a quid on for me—if—if I'm not available.'

'I'm afraid I don't know any bookmakers,' you say.

'Never mind,' says Mr Green. 'Perhaps I'll be able to do it myself. What d'you think?'

'Do I think you'll get off, do you mean? Well——'

Mr Green holds up his hand to stop you.

'Don't answer. Bad luck to answer that question. If you say "no" it's depressing, and if you say "yes" it's a disappointment later.'

'Do tell me what you're charged with,' you say.

'Now that's a point,' says Mr Green. 'I wonder if they've framed it right.' He pulls the indictment out of his pocket. 'But they must have,' he goes on. 'They couldn't have made the same mistake twice.'

At that moment a prison officer comes to the door and says that his Lordship would like to know if you're ready.

'Well——' you begin.

'I think you'd better come up, sir, and tell the judge how long you'll be.'

Very red in the face you go up the stairs and into counsel's row. The judge beams at you.

'Are you sure you're quite ready, Mr Green? I don't want to hurry you in any way.'

Almost scarlet you manage to say :

'I'm afraid I'm not quite ready, my Lord, as a matter of fact.'

'That's quite all right, Mr Green. Take your time. D'you think another ten minutes will be enough?'

'I'm not sure, my Lord,' you say truthfully.

The judge's smile contracts a little.

'Will you be good enough to tell me how long you do want? You've had half-an-hour already.'

'Well, my Lord,' you begin—and then you falter. You simply have no idea how long to ask for. One of your neighbours pulls your gown.

'Ask for a week's adjournment,' he says. 'Say there may be a question of witnesses.'

Entrance to a court at the Old Bailey
or
'Fancy meeting you here'

You take the advice.

'I see,' says the judge. 'How many witnesses?'

'I'm not sure,' you say truthfully.

'Which part of the country do they come from?' says the judge.

'I'm not sure,' you repeat.

'Mr Green—is there anything you are sure of?'

'Not at the moment, my Lord, I'm afraid. I'm having some difficulty in getting my client's instructions.'

You're improving already, you see.

'I'm not going to have the Court played about with,' says the judge. 'If you genuinely want an adjournment to call witnesses you shall have it. If you give me your word that it may be necessary to call one or more witnesses who are not in Court today I'll grant you an adjournment, but not otherwise.'

You say nothing.

'Well,' says the judge.

'Might I go and see my client again?' you ask.

'Oh, very well—I suppose so,' says the judge. 'But don't be more than five minutes.'

'Thank you, my Lord,' you say, and hurry into the dock and down the stairs to your client again. For a beginner you have done remarkably well so far, but what is going to happen now?

'Mr Green,' you say, 'are there any witnesses you need for your defence?'

'Witnesses eh?' says Mr Green. 'That's a new idea. I've never had any before. What d'you want them to say?'

Well, somehow or other you deal with the position and no doubt Mr Green is in the end duly convicted in spite of your impassioned speech to the jury, in which you have probably reminded them several times that they are men and women of the world. Why exactly that should make a jury less likely to convict a prisoner will always remain uncertain, but it is a very popular cliché with some advocates. After Mr Green has been sentenced, he asks if he may have permission to speak to you about an appeal. With a vision of yourself addressing the Court of Appeal you hurry down the stairs again.

'Well,' says Mr Green. 'That's that. Thank you very much. It was my fault really. It was the foreman of the jury. He bites his finger nails. If I'd seen it earlier, I'd have told you to object to him. However, no good crying over spilt milk. I wouldn't be doing anything else if I did.'

'You want to appeal?' you say.

'Not likely,' says Mr Green, 'and have an extra three months while I'm waiting. What d'you take me for? Three years was quite reasonable, anyway. He's a good judge that. Should go a long way.'

'But what did you want to see me for?'

'Oh—of course—thanks. I told you—my memory's not what it was. It's that seller at Catterick. If you go to Tommy Parsons, of 15 Possett Lane, S.E.21, he'll put it on for you.'

'But I'm not sure,' you begin—

'Come on,' says Mr Green. 'He won't bite you. And you can send me my share of the winnings, you know. The governor will keep it for me. You ought to get ten to one—hundred to eight even.'

You're rather sorry for Mr Green but you're not going to start backing horses or calling on Mr Green's racing friends. Before you can say anything, Mr Green holds up his hand :

'Now, don't say anything. Keep it as a surprise.

Then, if the horse turns up (we hear about these things you know—*and* premium bond numbers) if it turns up, I'll be able to wonder whether you put ıt on—that'll give me something to think about—and if it don't, then I can hope you didn't. It might be a nice surprise, you never know.'

At that moment the prison officer returns.

'Green,' he says, 'you're wanted back again. And you, sir. The judge forgot to sentence him on the third count.'

'I said *nice* surprise,' says Mr Green. Then he turns to you.

'Don't look so worried. I shan't get any more. It'll all be concurrent. They do this sometimes—when they're in a hurry for tea. Only goes to show—more haste less speed. Up we go, chum.'

23 *Women at the Bar*

ALTHOUGH, for the sake of simplicity, this book has apparently been addressed to men, it is, of course, intended equally for women. It is, however, only fair to warn prospective women barristers that there is probably no profession where it is harder for them to make headway than at the Bar. There is no good reason to think that this is due to any lack of ability on the part of women or to any relevant difference in the make-up of a woman from that of a man.

It is possible that one reason for the present lack of success among women is because few women with the necessary qualities have come to the Bar, but the main reason is probably lack of opportunity. There is still almost overwhelming prejudice against women both at the Bar itself and among solicitors and among the public. In consequence, it is extremely difficult for a woman to find a vacancy in chambers. It is difficult enough for a man, but far worse for a woman. Moreover, on the whole, solicitors do not care to brief women and the public still appears shy of entrusting its fate to a woman.

There is no justifiable reason for this. A woman with the necessary qualities who is able to give the required time to the job should be able to be just as successful as a man. It is nevertheless true that very few have achieved success, and it does not appear that the road is becoming much easier, although the fact that there is now one woman High Court judge, three women Circuit judges and one woman magistrate should give a little encouragement to women.

But unless a girl has an overwhelming desire to overcome all these difficulties, it is strongly recommended that, before she embarks on her legal studies, she should make enquiries as to the possibility of her being taken as a pupil in suitable chambers. The great importance of pupillage has already been stressed, but, for the reasons mentioned, it is even more important for a woman. Unless she has quite outstanding qualities and luck as well it is almost impossible for a woman to succeed unless she can find a vacancy in really good chambers, and many chambers will not accept women. Although no one is going to promise a vacancy for a pupil three years ahead, it would seem a reasonable precaution to make enquiries and consult friends about the possibility of pupillage before the expense and time of a legal education are incurred. It is far easier for a woman to succeed as a solicitor and, if a girl wishes to adopt the law as a profession and is not prepared to incur the serious risk of failing at the Bar, it is recommended that she should become one. There is no reason why she should not succeed.

The object of this chapter is certainly not to criticise the ability of women nor is it intended to criticse those chambers who will not accept women pupils or women members. There are intelligible reasons for this, whether a person agrees with them or not. The object is not to criticise, but to set down the cold, cruel facts so that the pioneers—for that is what they still are—may realise that their road is even more full of obstructions than that of their male counterparts. It they do decide to take the risk, every word of advice contained in this book is intended equally for them, except that they have no front stud to conceal with their bands.

Lady Barrister
or
'What I really feel in this case is'

24 *Without Prejudice*

THE words 'Without Prejudice' are often misunderstood by the public and sometimes by lawyers. Insurance company officials use them so often that it would not be altogether surprising if one of them, on being asked during the marriage service if he will take the lady to be his wife, were to say: 'I will, without prejudice.'

There are only two senses in which the words can properly be used. In any discussions for a compromise of an alleged legal liability either party may say or write that the discussions are 'without prejudice.' Once these words are used by either party in such discussions (whether conducted in writing or by word of mouth) neither side can refer to the discussions or produce any letters relating to them in Court, without the consent of the other side. This is an absolute rule in civil cases. It will sometimes be a temptation to you to read something from a 'without prejudice' letter. You must always resist the temptation.

But, although no one may refer to the contents of such letters in Court without the consent of the other side, you must not take an unfair advantage of this fact, and, if your opponent should try to do so, the judge will uphold you when you point out what is happening. For example, suppose that A had written to B alleging that B had promised to do something for him, and that B replied at once in a letter headed 'without prejudice' that he denied making the promise, but that in order to save the expense of litigation he would be prepared to make a compromise of some kind. Suppose also that this was the only letter in which B had denied making the promise. If in these circumstances A's counsel, knowing that B's 'without prejudice' letter could not be read to the Court, opened the case to the judge by saying that B had never denied the promise, he would be acting unfairly and, if necessary, the 'without prejudice' letter would be looked at by the judge. But such a situation ought not to arise and it is not a real exception to the rule that in civil cases 'without prejudice' correspondence cannot be looked at without the consent of *both* sides.

But the protection for 'without prejudice' discussions or correspondence only arises if there is a genuine attempt by one side or both to arrive at a compromise. If there is no such attempt the use of the words 'without prejudice' will have no effect whatsoever. For example :

Dear Sir,
Unless you send me £100 by tomorrow I will tell your wife what I know about you.
Without prejudice,
Yours sincerely,
A. Wellwisher.
P.S. Put the money under the doormat.

This letter would in no way be privileged from production in Court, and it illustrates the further point that this question of privilege for 'without prejudice' documents or correspondence does not apply in any way to criminal proceedings. You cannot murder anyone or steal from them without prejudice. And in criminal proceedings all your letters can be produced as evidence, however much they may be marked 'without prejudice.'

G

The other sense of the term 'without prejudice' is quite different. It often occurs in contracts or correspondence. For example: 'Without prejudice to the question of liability, we are prepared to agree the damage at £100.'

This is not a 'without prejudice' letter. It means what it says. The agreement as to damage is not to prejudice the argument on liability. This is quite different from the first use of the words 'without prejudice,' where they are in effect a protective label.

Sometimes solicitors will conduct two sets of correspondence at the same time, one 'without prejudice' and one with. The 'with prejudice' correspondence is known in those circumstances as 'open.' You may be consulted about such correspondence and indeed you may be drafting the letters for your solicitor to send. If so, be careful that you don't confuse the two sets and introduce something from a 'without prejudice' letter into an 'open' reply.

A few lawyers still think that, when a case has been decided, 'without prejudice' correspondence can be read to the judge on the issue of costs. This is quite wrong. Without the consent of both sides, 'without prejudice' correspondence can never be read to the judge at any stage *in the court proceedings to which they relate.* Normally in another action altogether they can be read freely. The only reason for the rule is to facilitate settlements and, as a person might think it would be a sign of weakness to discuss compromise, he can, if he uses the protective label, do so freely for the purpose of settling those proceedings. But the letters are not otherwise privileged, and they could form the basis of a libel action if they contained unjustified defamatory matter.

The Crypt at the Law Courts
or
Refreshers

25 *General Rules and Conclusion*

THERE are two vital principles to which you must adhere from the start. Never in any circumstances must you deceive or attempt to deceive the Court, or directly or indirectly encourage witnesses to do so. Nor must you ever deliberately tell an untruth or a half-truth to your opponent. Fight your cases as hard as you can but never in the heat of battle allow yourself to deviate from these two principles. You will find temptation enough to do so in your early days. Every now and then you will lose a case and perhaps a client by keeping to your principles. Such cases and clients are well lost, though you may not think so at the time. One thing you can be assured of—that the use of improper or unsatisfactory methods will never get you to the top of the tree. If you're going to get there, you will do so without them, and, if you're not, an unsavoury reputation will keep you down, not send you up. Judges and barristers soon get to know whom they can trust. In fact a very large majority of the Bar can be trusted implicitly, but there is a small minority who, while not indulging in practices which are likely to get themselves disbarred, sail fairly near the wind. And there is a tiny minority who are dishonest and would be disbarred if found out.

One of the temptations you will find it hard to resist in your early days is the temptation to persuade your client to tell, not a lie, but a slightly different story from the one he originally told. And there can be worse things than that. For example :

YOUNG COUNSEL : But if he looked both ways he must have seen the defendant's car. The road was quite straight.

SOLICITOR'S CLERK : But he couldn't have seen to the left if there'd been a pantechnicon drawn up at the corner. He'd have to have moved out beyond it.

YOUNG COUNSEL : But he hasn't said anything about a pantechnicon being there.

SOLICITOR'S CLERK (winking) : No, he hasn't—not yet. But he hasn't said there wasn't one.

Now if this were your second brief, and the first one ever sent you by this particular client, what would you do? Is it not fair to say that at the best you would say :

YOUNG COUNSEL : You will be sure to see that he doesn't say it if it isn't true.

SOLICITOR'S CLERK : You trust me.

Later the pantechnicon appears in your client's statement in all its glory. You see him in conference.

YOUNG COUNSEL : Are you really sure about this pantechnicon?

CLIENT : Quite sure.

YOUNG COUNSEL : Why didn't you mention it in your first statement?

CLIENT : I'd forgotten about it.

YOUNG COUNSEL : It seems an odd thing to forget.

CLIENT : Have you never forgotten anything?

YOUNG COUNSEL : Of course I have—but you made a long statement to Mr Jones here and you said nothing whatever about the pantechnicon.

SOLICITOR'S CLERK : If I may intervene here, sir—I took the statement rather hurriedly. I had another appointment, and I'm afraid I rather rushed the client.

I must take the blame for the mistake entirely. I'm extremely sorry, sir.

Unfortunately for your client he had made a statement to the police just after the accident in which also, curiously enough, there was no mention of any pantechnicon. But perhaps the policeman had another appointment too and rather hurried him? If he did, he doesn't say so in the witness-box. Your client's evidence is not accepted by the judge. The truth has a nasty habit of coming out. It is not a bad thing to remind some lay clients of this.

There is an infinite number of variations of the scene just described. Some are less obviously dishonest and indeed less dishonest. But you must make up your mind here and now that you are going to lay down a hard and fast rule as to what can be done and what can't be done, and don't compromise with yourself on the subject. When in doubt consult someone of experience.

It is not suggested for a moment that the example given is a regular occurrence, or that legal executives or solicitors' clerks as a whole are not entirely honest. They are. But there are a few who are not too scrupulous. Lack of scruple may result in conduct which is merely rather unsatisfactory or, at the other end of the scale, which is grossly improper. It is when dealing with this small but real minority that you have to be on your guard.

Another rule, which is important but nothing like so important, relates to interruptions in Court. Quite reputable members of the Bar interrupt too often. Remember that it is unfair to interrupt merely for the purpose of putting your opponent off his stroke. The best advocates only interrupt when there is a real reason for it. Indeed they often refrain from interrupting when an intervention would be justified. If you only make justifiable interruptions, it will soon become obvious to the judge that you only intervene when they are really called for. Such a reputation is obviously very helpful to you and to your clients. Conversely, the man who is always interrupting unnecessarily annoys the judge. Often a justifiable interruption is in fact unnecessary. So don't always stand strictly on your legal rights. Before you interrupt think what is to be gained by the interruption. If nothing worth having, don't make it.

Here is a small tip which you may find useful when you have a case before a jury. If you are appearing for the defendant try not to say anything in the course of the plaintiff's counsel's opening, or during the examination of his first witness. And try to make the start of your cross-examination an effective one. The result of your silence will be that the jury will be hearing your voice for the first time when you start to cross-examine. A new voice may be a tonic to them and in any event they want to hear what you are like. If you've already said quite a lot (none of it probably helping your case in the least) there will be no novelty to hold the jury's attention when you get up to cross-examine. Indeed if you are one of the interrupting sort, one of the jury may be saying to himself :

'Here's this fellow again. Judging by the amount he talks during the other fellow's case we're in for a marathon. Oh well—it's a public duty. Wonder how Jean's getting on at the interview. I wonder if we'll finish in time to get to Lord's. What's that he's saying? Oh—gosh—he's said all that before. Jean must be at the interview by now. I wonder what's happening?'

Always be scrupulously polite both to your opponent and to witnesses. A quiet cross-examination is far more effective than a fiery one. A rude one is always likely to annoy the judge or the jury, or both, and it is contrary to the rules of your profession. You have an absolute privilege for anything you say. You cannot be sued for slander for anything you say in Court. It is, therefore, incumbent on you not to abuse your privilege by being rude to people. It may be necessary to put the most unpleasant allegations to a witness, but it is never necessary to put them rudely.

Another thing to avoid is comment on a witness's evidence during that evidence. The cliché—'So that's what you say, is it?' when he says something that doesn't suit your case, is to be avoided at all costs. The same applies to 'we shall see.' In cross-examination your sole right and duty is to ask questions, not to comment on the answers.

One mistake is frequently made in cross-examination, even by experienced practitioners. They go on too long. Having obtained the answer they want they are so pleased that they go on pressing the witness. Sometimes the result is that the witness sees the point and promptly changes his first answer. For example, in the sausages case, suppose the plaintiff's counsel had failed to elicit from the witness that sausages were mentioned at the interview. The defendant's counsel ought not to cross-examine the witness at all on that subject. But some inexperienced counsel might well not resist the temptation of saying :

'You're quite sure nothing else was mentioned?'

Whereupon the witness scratches his head and eventually says :

'Well—only the sausages.'

(Collapse of defendant's counsel.)

That, of course, is an extreme example and few

experienced practitioners would make such a glaring mistake. But they often make it in less obvious cases. Economy in cross-examination should be your watchword.

When I was a County Court Judge I once tried a case where the plaintiff was claiming damages from the defendant in an accident case. The plaintiff's case was that he was driving up a hill on the proper side of the road when the defendant came very fast in the other direction from the top of the hill which had a curve on it, was unable to keep to his proper side, came right across the road and caused a head-on collision.

The plaintiff called in support of his case a man who was wheeling a bicycle up the hill who said that he witnessed the accident, that he saw the defendant come very fast over the top of the hill and swerve across the road and run into the plaintiff. This witness gave his evidence extremely well and he was eventually cross-examined by experienced counsel. The cross-examination went as follows :

COUNSEL : Mr Jones, you say my client came over the hill at a very fast speed.

THE WITNESS : Yes.

COUNSEL : I think you said he was going at about 60 miles an hour.

THE WITNESS : Yes, 60 or thereabouts.

COUNSEL : Are you a good judge of speed?

THE WITNESS : Yes I am.

COUNSEL : Do you drive a motor car or motor cycle?

THE WITNESS : No, I don't.

That was the time for counsel to stop, but he did not. He asked a further question.

COUNSEL : What are you, Mr Jones?

THE WITNESS : I'm an engine driver.

As I said, the counsel concerned was experienced and his face did not show what he felt, but he must have kicked himself very hard for asking that further question. In fact his asking the question did not affect the case, because, if he had not asked it, I would have done so, but it's about the best example I know of one question too many being asked in cross-examination.

As long as you are fighting a case never give up. This does not mean that you should not try to arrive at a compromise if it is pretty plain that you are going to lose. But, as long as you are actually fighting, keep at it. Not by repeating yourself time and again, and not by taking hopeless points, but by taking the best point or points there may be in your favour and hammering away at them. If there are absolutely none, the case should probably not have been fought at all. In your early days you will in all probability want to drop your brief and run away from time to time, and you will pray that judgment may be given against you as quickly as possible and the agony be over. But don't give in. Never turn tail and run. And see that you call the evidence that may be in your favour. And don't hurry it through just because you know you're going to lose and want to get it over.

It is probable that you will lose cases owing to your inexperience and ignorance. On the way home you will suddenly realise something you might have done. You will then try to convince yourself that it would not have done any good anyway. Finally you will decide that no one could have won the case. Well—what you say to your friends and relatives is a matter for your own conscience, but what you say to yourself is important. You must profit by your mistakes and, if you deliberately shut your eyes to them, they will have been made in vain. It is an imperfect world. There is no absolute justice in any country. Cases which ought to be won will continue to be lost. There is no one at the Bar or on the Bench who has not in his time lost a case which could or should have been won. But those who succeed acknowledge their failures, at any rate to themselves.

Always keep your temper. Occasionally a show of indignation may be justified and serve you in good stead. But once your outburst is uncontrolled it may lead to more harm than good. You must always be in command of your words and you can't be if you lose your temper. There was a famous barrister who was renowned both as advocate and as lawyer. His only fault as an advocate was that he had a tendency to lose his temper. He was well aware of this. On one occasion another well-known barrister was trying to annoy him by making *sotto voce* remarks to him when he was examining a witness during a difficult case. He stopped his examination and turning quietly to his opponent said :

'You're a very nasty little boy but I'm not going to let you make me lose my temper.'

He kept his temper, and won his case.

The importance of not putting serious allegations to opposing witnesses without being as sure as possible of your ground has already been mentioned. This advice of course equally applies to every question you ask in cross-examination, but the harm likely to be done to your client is usually greater if a serious allegation is put to a witness without justification. In your early days you will certainly have questions suggested to you by your solicitor or his representative while you are actually on your feet cross-examining. Be very, very careful about those questions and, if you're not sure about them, don't hesitate to ask the judge for a few moments' grace in which to whisper to your client about the matter. Very, very occasionally it might even be necessary to ask for a few minutes' adjournment. Naturally a judge is not going to like a case being broken off in the middle like that, but, if the circumstances justify the application, you should make it.

'My Lord, I have just received some information which may be of great importance. Would your Lordship give me a few minutes' indulgence to take instructions on the matter before I continue cross-examining the witness?'

If it turns out to be a red herring, come back and say so and apologise. But it is much better to take care, even at the risk of irritating the judge, than to put unfounded allegations to a witness.

In a case many years ago a witness was giving evidence. Counsel who was cross-examining him was suddenly informed in a whisper that a police constable who happened to be in Court said that he felt sure that the man had a criminal conviction for perjury. Counsel's case was that the witness was not only telling lies but that he had removed the ignition key of a motor car with a view to giving evidence that a man's motor car was outside a certain woman's house all night. If, therefore, it was possible to show that the witness had been convicted of perjury, it would have been of tremendous value. On the other hand to put the definite question—'Have you been convicted of perjury?' would be terribly dangerous if the information was not true. There was no time to obtain a certificate of the conviction if there was one. Normally you should always have a certificate in your possession if you are

The Jury
or
There's always a chance

going to suggest to a man that he has been convicted. On this occasion, when he came to an appropriate stage in his cross-examination, counsel went on as follows:

COUNSEL: Perhaps you didn't understand the last question. Perhaps you're not used to giving evidence?

No answer.

COUNSEL: I said—perhaps you're not used to giving evidence. Perhaps you've never been in a Court before?

No answer.

COUNSEL: Well—have you been in a Court before?

WITNESS (reluctantly): Yes.

COUNSEL: Oh? A Court like this?

WITNESS: No.

COUNSEL: Oh—what sort of Court?

WITNESS: A police court.

COUNSEL: And what were you doing there? Appearing as a witness?

WITNESS: No.

COUNSEL: Oh—what was it then?

WITNESS: I was charged.

COUNSEL: What with?

WITNESS: Making a false declaration.

COUNSEL: What happened?

WITNESS: I was fined.

COUNSEL: Did you plead guilty or not guilty?

WITNESS: Guilty.

COUNSEL: So you had made a false declaration?

WITNESS: Yes.

COUNSEL: And was that your only appearance in Court?

WITNESS: No.

COUNSEL: What was the other occasion?

WITNESS: In the police court.

COUNSEL: What happened that time?

WITNESS : I was convicted of making a false declaration.

COUNSEL : And had you pleaded guilty or not guilty?

WITNESS : Guilty.

It is, of course, not desirable to have to obtain the evidence in this way. But in the particular circumstances of that case it was the only method open to counsel, unless he applied for an adjournment. And you will observe that, until the witness's actual admission, no serious allegation was put to the witness. If the witness had said that he had never been in Court before, the line of cross-examination would, of course, have been discontinued, and no adverse comment could have been made about the question being asked.

That is not a normal line of cross-examination for you to adopt. It was a very rare case. But you will note the care taken by counsel, in spite of the fact that the information came from a police constable. There was no certificate of conviction, and the information might have been wrong.

Re-examination of a witness is for the purpose of clearing up something in cross-examination which requires further explanation or which may have left a false impression. Occasionally there can be a very useful re-examination, but for the most part it is unnecessary. As often as not, counsel feel that they ought to re-examine but all they elicit is something that's already been said. Get the reputation for only re-examining when it is really necessary.

There are one or two mistakes which even experienced practitioners make but which stamp the makers as either inexperienced or as below a certain standard. They are only important inasmuch as they give you away.

For example :

    (i) The second 'e' in 'condition precēdent' is long and is pronounced as in 'preceding'. Many people pronounce it in the same way as in 'judicial precedent' where, of course, it is short.

    (ii) The Scottish reports Session Cases should never be referred to as Sessions Cases.

    (iii) Don't refer to the 'learned justices' or to the 'learned clerk' in a County Court. Only qualified lawyers are entitled to be called 'learned.' If you're not sure whether a person is qualified (as in the case of an associate in the High Court, who sometimes is and sometimes is not) by all means err on the side of courtesy. But some practitioners think that they ought to call everyone 'learned.' It has been said that counsel once referred to 'the learned usher,' but this may be apocryphal.

    (iv) Get your pronunciation of judges' names and legal Latin correct. If, for example, you refer to Lopes L. J. as though his name rhymes with ropes, it will sadden a judge in much the same way as the pronunciation of awry to rhyme with story will depress a teacher of English.

Learn all about costs. Apart from the fact that this will endear you to your solicitor client, the costs are sometimes the most important thing in a case. They even may exceed the amount of the claim, particularly in the County Court. You must, therefore, know the rules about costs and be prepared to quote them to the Court. Some years ago a young barrister appeared before a Registrar in a County Court.

'What do the rules say about this question of costs?' he was asked.

'I'm afraid I don't know,' the young man replied. 'You see I was only called last night. I was told that there would be nothing to do except ask for judgment.'

Well, that young man can be excused, but not the system which then permitted him to appear.

A majority of advocates clear their throats or give a slight cough when they get up to cross-examine a witness. It is a sign of nervousness. You will notice that you do it yourself, but you can soon rid yourself of the habit. If you really need to clear your throat do so when you see that the examination-in-chief is nearing its end.

When you've finished examining or cross-examining a witness, don't *automatically* turn to your solicitor or his representative and whisper to him : 'Is there anything else?' This is normally done, not because the advocate wants to know, but as a kind of cover for himself. Get your case up properly and you will require no cover. If you really think that you may have missed something and that the person you are speaking to may have something worth while to suggest, of course ask him or her. But the question is often addressed to a diminutive clerk, not long out of swaddling clothes, who is only there to hold the papers and knows nothing about the case whatever. The fact that you ask the child the question shows lack of confidence in yourself. And be quite sure of this : even if it is not a child that you ask but a full-grown solicitor, asking the question will not in any way relieve you of your responsibilities—and it is your responsibility to cover all the necessary points, not your solicitor's or his representative's.

As far as possible know your judge. Many have their own foibles. There was a County Court judge who hated people saying 'with respect' to him. So those who knew him left it out. Occasionally you may find one with an inferiority complex. There was one such judge who was quick to suspect that you did not think he knew some legal principle. You were probably quite right, but it was important not to let him see it. Great tact was necessary. It was no use saying:

'As your Lordship well knows,' if you said it in a way which made it plain that you were quite sure that he didn't know.

Whatever a judge's foibles, don't be browbeaten by him. Always be polite, but be firm too. Stand up for yourself and above all for your client. Occasionally a judge will make an unjustifiable criticism of your client. Don't hesitate to protest firmly but courteously. If he's a good judge and you're right, he'll apologise. If he's a bad judge you may have taught him something, and at least you will have protected your client.

A word about the Press. You probably know that you must never give interviews to the Press. Although you may derive pleasure and advertisement from reports in the newspapers of cases which you have conducted, you must not take any steps to try to ensure publication of such reports. Human nature being what it is, if your uncle is editor of the *London Daily*, he may get reporters of his to cover your cases. You cannot prevent him and I don't suppose you'd want to. But you can at least suggest to him that he doesn't go too far, as otherwise it may be thought that it was done by arrangement with you. So it would be, if you notified him in advance of the cases you were doing and where and when you were doing them, knowing that he would have them reported. You must resist such temptations.

As you get more work in the High Court one of the law reporters (they are all qualified barristers) may ask you if there's anything for him in a case you're conducting. That means that he wants to know if the case is likely to involve a point of law which is worth reporting. There is a type of barrister who always answers this question in the affirmative, and who would follow it up by a long and tedious statement about the case if the law reporter did not hurriedly withdraw. The law reporters know this type all too well. Don't become one of them. If there really is something to report in your case, of course say so. But don't pretend that there is when there isn't. It won't do you any good and you'd be horrified to hear what the law reporters said about you among themselves if you become one of the type just mentioned.

Finally, never do anything which you would object to your opponent doing. Be absolutely honest with the Court, your opponents and your clients.

The object of this book has been to give you a rough idea of what is meant by going to the Bar and to make some suggestions to help you to succeed. It has been very far from exhaustive but it will not have been without some value to you if you have started to get some idea of what is meant by a leading question, and if you are now determined never to accept anything that is said to you without being satisfied as to the principle behind it and without *looking it up*. It is very easy to get into the way of sloppy thinking. You will certainly not get anywhere near the top if you indulge in it.

It is too difficult to resist the temptation to end with

the words of a fictional Treasurer of an Inn, addressing young men and women who were about to be called to the Bar :

'I wish you all the success you deserve,' he said. 'I am sure you will have it and I hope that that thought will not depress too many of you.'

Appendix

LOOK THESE UP

(1) Since the Rent Restriction Acts were first passed in the first World War there must have been hundreds or thousands of judgments given against statutory tenants for 'mesne profits' up to the date of judgment. Were those judgments permissible? Can you order mesne profits against a statutory tenant? Most text books say that mesne profits are damages for trespass. But a statutory tenant is not a trespasser until the Court orders him to go and the time which he has been given expires. How can you then order mesne profits against him for a period before the date of the Order? All right, you say, order the same sum as arrears of rent. But you can't give judgment, can you, for any sum which became due after the issue of the summons except mesne profits? That is a statutory exception to the rule that the cause of action must exist at the date of the issue of the proceedings. Well—what is the answer to it? Either the judgments are all wrong or the text books are wrong when they say that mesne profits *are* damages for trespass. Perhaps the answer is that although the expression mesne profits includes damages for trepass it does not exclude a claim for money due for use and occupation. Anyway, look it up.

(2) If a plaintiff recovers £500 from a defendant and the defendant has paid the whole amount into Court before the hearing but it is not accepted, what is the proper form of judgment? You will find cases where judgment is given for the plaintiff for £500 with costs

up to the date of payment in and judgment for the defendant for costs after that date. Is that right? A lot of people will tell you that it is, but it is not. Look it up.

(3) What is an 'equitable set-off?' If a landlord sues for rent and the tenant has a valid claim for damages for breach of a covenant to repair, can the tenant set off the damages, when assessed, against the claim for rent? If the owner of a bombed site lets part of it to the owner of a lorry and the lorry is lost owing to the negligence of the landlord, can the tenant set off the value of the lorry against the landlord's claim for arrears of rent?

There are conflicting cases on this subject.[1] What is the answer? It is not just a technical point. It may turn out to be very important indeed on the issue of costs.

(4) In standard works of high authority you will find a Statement of Claim in an action for goods sold and delivered in the following form :

The plaintiff's claim is for £500 being the price of goods sold and delivered by the plaintiff to the defendant.

Particulars

1957
1 January. To 500 skins at £1 each...............£500
            And the Plaintiff claims £500.

That form of pleading may be hallowed by antiquity but is it right? Can you think of any criticism which can be made of it?

Must not every pleading show a good cause of action? Merely to sell and deliver goods to a person does not create a cause of action. There is no allegation in this

[1] After this was written in 1958 there was an important decision of the Court of Appeal on the subject. What case does the Court appear to have overruled without mentioning it in the judgment?

pleading that the price has not been paid. Although the law assumes that a debt once proved to exist continues to exist until the contrary is proved, the law does not assume that if a price is payable on delivery (as in default of agreement it is) it has not been paid. If there were any assumption it would be that a man discharges his obligations as and when he should, until the contrary is proved. Be that as it may, there is no assumption by the law that a price is not paid when it is due to be paid. Surely then the pleading should contain the words : 'Which has not been paid by the defendant to the plaintiff either in whole or in part' ?

Whether the pleading is right or wrong, this criticism is one that ought to occur to you if you have understood the rules of pleading. It may be that this particular form of pleading had its origin many years ago and can be justified in some way historically, having regard to the forms of pleading before the Judicature Act (1873).

You will find other examples of this kind of thing in forms of precedents, and, if you blindly follow such forms in simple matters of this kind which are never going to be challenged, you will find yourself doing it in more complicated matters where it will be challenged.

Index